The 5th & Ultimate SECRET DIARIES OF JOHN MAJOR

Published in Great Britain
by Private Eye Productions Ltd
6 Carlisle Street, London W1V 5RG
in association with Corgi Books

© 1996 Pressdram Ltd
ISBN 0 552 14523 8

Designed by Bridget Tisdall
Printed in England by
Ebenezer Baylis & Son Ltd, Worcester

Corgi Books are published by Transworld Publishers Ltd
61–63 Uxbridge Road, Ealing, London W5 5SA
in Australia by Transworld Publishers (Australia) Pty, Ltd
15–23 Helles Avenue, Moorebank, NSW 2170
and in New Zealand by Transworld Publishers (N.Z.) Ltd
3 William Pickering Drive, Albany, Auckland

2 4 6 8 10 9 7 5 3 1

The 5th & Ultimate SECRET DIARY OF JOHN MAJOR

**Illustrated by
Caroline Holden**

PRIVATE EYE · CORGI

September

Monday

I have come back from my holiday in a very good mood indeed. I am on top of the world. From now on everything is going to be different. For a start I am going to take over running the government by myself. My policy is one of:

● leading from the front
● hands-on
● top-down
● me totally in charge
● Mr Heseltine not.

All my ministers are going to be told that from now on it is me who is going to have the ideas. In future they should come to me before they do or say anything. In this way, we shall draw a line under everything that has happened up till now and I shall win the next election single-handed i.e.

● hands down
● top off
● on my own
● ... er...

l that's it.

Tuesday

I decided to begin my new style of government by telling Mr Heseltine in no uncertain terms how things are going to be from now on. Unfortunately the red light outside his door

was on all morning, so
I could not get in to
see him until late
afternoon.

I think he is losing
his grip. When I went
up to his desk he
scratched his head
and said "Remind me,
who are you?" I felt
sorry for him. He is
obviously getting very
old. One cannot have
such a man running
the country, which he
is not, because I am.
Oh yes.

I was just trying to tell him that I am now the hands-off
eyes-down top dog on the block, when he pushed an invoice
into my hand saying "Get Fatty Clarke to pay this, will you?
Apparently I've libelled some grotty little journalist." Usually
libel works the other way round which proves that Mr
Heseltine is not as clever as everyone says. "The bill is for
£86,000," he told me. Obviously I will have to explain to Mr
Heseltine my plan to take over the government when he is
less busy.

Wednesday

Today was a very historic day indeed. I have invaded
Bosnia. Luckily I remembered that when they put the new
door into Mr Heseltine's office, they had put my *Daily
Telegraph* map of the world in the cupboard. So I got it out
and spread it out on my desk, like Mr Churchill in the war. In
my lunch break I went to Ryman's and bought some little
pins with coloured tops to show where all our bombs had
fallen. While I was laying them out Mr Portaloo came in, very
excited. "It is a historic day," he said. "I know," I replied, "I
have already said that in my diary." That put him in his
place, and showed who is in charge, i.e me and not Mr
Heseltine, and certainly not Mr Portaloo who is only Mr
Heseltine's defence secretary. "By the way," I asked him,
"why have we decided to invade now?" "Everyone agrees that
it is the only possible course of action," he said. "Then why
have we waited three years to do it?" I asked, quick as a flash.
Mr Portaloo looked very embarrassed, and said that it wasn't

his idea. He was only obeying orders from above. "Ah," I said, "Mr Heseltine?" "No," he said,"even higher than that. From Mr Clinton."

Thursday

I am very glad to see from the *Daily Telegraph* that our bombers have all succeeded in hitting important Serb targets. These include:

1. Group of fir trees near to Serb positions.
2. Important cowshed of vital strategic value to the enemy, containing 2 cows (probably *Serb*).
3. 1 very important wheatfield.

This is a very good start, but we must keep up the bombing until the Serbs agree to the Vance-Owen plan (revised 1993, 1994, 1995), the details of which Mr Hurd was the only person ever to understand. I went to look for it in my cupboard, but there was only a note saying "All important files removed to office of M.H."

Friday

Today is an even more historic day. It marks the first anniversary of my greatest achievement, bringing a lasting peace to Northern Ireland. My lasting peace has already lasted a year, which in my judgement is a not inconsiderably long time. As I told my wife Norman over our breakfast of Multi Cheerios and EC-approved square croissants, "the longer it lasts, the more likely it is to last longer". "Just like you" she said, which in my view was a considerably silly remark. Fortunately my brilliant new party chairman Mr Mawhinney came in with some very cheering news. He was waving a copy of the *Daily Mail* with the headline "Blair Finished — Poll Tonic For Tories". This clearly showed that Labour's lead had been dramatically cut from 57 points

to only 56. And a half. Mr Mawhinney thought it was all due to his tough speech about Labour councils putting up statues of hippopotamuses. But I knew that it was really thanks to my new top-down policy i.e. driving in the fast lane with the top down, my hands on the wheel and no one in the back seat telling me what to do, particularly not Mr Heseltine. The result of the next election now seems inevitable.

Saturday

Mr Mawhinney has been accused of "running scared" because he is trying to get a different seat at the next election.

"That's not true," he told me, "I am entirely confident in our electoral appeal. I just want to prove that Tories like me can win safe seats as well as marginal ones." I was greatly reassured by this.

Sunday

Mr Blair has stolen yet another of my not inconsiderably brilliant ideas i.e. telling his party to back him or else they will lose the election. When I mentioned this to Mr Portaloo on his way in to see Mr Heseltine he said, "Tony Blair should be careful. A Party can end up backing the leader and then losing anyway."

This was very supportive of him and shows that my top-down approach is beginning to work its way up as far as Mr Portaloo.

Monday

It is all over for Mr Blair. A top-secret document has been leaked to the newspapers saying that Labour "have no ideas and are not fit to run the country". "Sounds familiar," said my wife Norman, when we were eating our bowls of Muroroa Atomic Muesli, a present from Mr Monsieur Chirac after I had sent him a letter of support for whatever it is he is doing. I have no idea what she meant, and it seemed to me an imprudent and unhelpful remark.

Tuesday

Mr Redwood, who I have now totally forgotten since he tried to steal my job, is not the only one to have a think-tank. Oh no. Today I have summoned the whole Cabinet to Chequers for a top-secret, top-down, hands-on conference, to come up with hundreds of brilliant ideas for winning the next election. Mr Mawhinney, my brilliant new party chairman, has been working on the agenda for our discussion. So far it reads:

1. How to win the election.

2. How to come up with hundreds of ideas for winning the election.

We had a very successful meeting which lasted all day, apart from lunch and tea.

Everyone was on tremendous form after their holidays and the discussion in my judgement showed that the Conservative party is by no means a spent force when it comes to having brilliant ideas. Oh no. In fact we were all thinking so hard that for hours nobody said a word. Finally I said: "What about having special tests for five-year-olds?" It was like a flash of lightning. Suddenly the whole way ahead became clear. Mr Blair and his so-called spin bowlers would never come up with an idea as brilliant as this in a thousand years. The next election is now in the bag.

Wednesday

This morning Mr Heseltine asked me to come through into his office. "Ah John," he said. "Your idea yesterday was a stroke of genius — the tests for five-year-olds, I mean. I think you should personally take the credit for it by announcing it yourself and telling the voters that this is very much your idea." This showed once again what a generous and loyal supporter he is, and that all the stories about him wanting to take over my job are not inconsiderably wide of the mark.

Thursday

This morning Mr Waldegrave asked to see me about "a very important personal matter". He was holding a copy of the *Sun* with the headline 'WALDEGRAVE'S TOFF RELATIVE TRIES TO TOP MISSUS'. "Do you think I should resign?" he asked, "because my brother has been accused of murder." "Don't be ridiculous," I said.

"If all of us had to resign because of our brothers, then I wouldn't be where I am today." I thought this would cheer him up, but for some reason he looked quite disappointed, and went out muttering something about how he had been hoping to "do a Hurd". This sounded very unpleasant and I don't know what he meant.

Friday

The session at Chequers was obviously much better than I thought. The papers are full of my Cabinet talking about their new ideas. They must have had them whilst I was busy in the *other* cabinet! (This is just my little joke, which was written for me by my brilliant "sound-bite" expert Mr Morris Norris.)

The ideas are as follows:

• Mr Howard is having special Boot Camps where young offenders will go to be booted. "It is nothing like the old short, sharp shock," he tells me. "This is a 'sharp, short shock'." And with a boot. To boot.

• Mr Waldegrave has thought of cutting welfare spending by 50%, so we can reduce taxes. Brilliant! Why has no one thought of this before? I think in my judgement I may have under-estimated Mr Waldegrave in making him serve the tea and biscuits — even though we may have to send his brother to one of the boot camps.

Saturday

I was in no small measure surprised to see in the *Daily Telegraph* that Mr Hurd has got a new job as a bank manager. My brother Terry rang me to ask whether I had seen the news. "You must be delighted," he said. "It means that after the next election you might be able to get your old job back." I told him that I was a very busy man and had no time to think about what I would do when we lose the next election, which we are not going to do anyway, because of my brilliant new policy of testing five-year-olds. "It's a good thing they didn't have tests in our day, John," he said, "otherwise you would never have got into Mrs Tremlett's reception class at primary. When you were five, you couldn't even remember the name of our squirrel, which you kept calling 'Cecil' when his name was 'Cyril'. It's all in my book, on page 186, if you want to buy the paperback, which will be out soon by the way." There are times when I think Mr Waldegrave's brother had the right idea when it comes to attacking people with breadknives.

Sunday

The idea of testing five-year-olds has been attacked by all the newspapers. It is clearly a useless idea and Mrs Shephard, the education secretary, should be ashamed of herself for thinking it up. Everyone says we are not spending enough money which is very unpopular, apparently. If Mr

Waldegrave has his way with his cuts we will have even *less* to spend! Perhaps I will put him back on biscuit duty after all.

The papers are also saying I put sun-cream on my goldfish because it is so hot. How ridiculous! As if anyone would do such a silly thing! I actually put *after-sun* on him because he was already burnt from the sun.

The real story they should be covering is the one that Mr Heseltine faxed to me about Mr Prescott. Mr Blair is obviously unable to control his deputy, who is a much stronger personality than he is and who is more popular in the party. I am glad I am not in *his* shoes.

Very Late Sunday Night (approx 10 p.m.)

Who says Britannia no longer rules the waves? Not me. Oh no. My wife Norman and I were tonight privileged to attend the Last Night of the Proms in a special box belonging to Mr Birt of the BBC. I had been told that Mr Birt was a boring man in glasses who was useless at his job. Not a bit of it! He and I got on very well from the start and discovered we had a lot in common.

The evening was organised by a Mr Drummond who had specially requested that there should be no noisy interruptions. Unfortunately a group of people chose to ignore these instructions and invaded the stage. One was dressed as a Teddy Boy and carried a saxophone (like my brother used to when he worked one Christmas at Woolworth's) and another, who looked like a homeless person on the underground, carried lots of drums. They both made a hideous noise and the conductor tried to stop them by waving his arms. Then a

Mr Birt-wistle (obviously a relation of Mr Birt) came forward and persuaded them to leave. We were very grateful and clapped a great deal.

Then the best thing of all happened. All the audience realised that I was in the box and began to sing "Land of Hope and Glory" like at the Tory Conference. Lots of them waved Union Jacks and cheered. Imagine Mr Blair getting such a standing ovation!

October

Saturday

Who says I am not in the heart of Europe! They have even named a whole island near Spain after me. It is now called Majorca, which is the Spanish for my name, and I flew there today for a very important summit meeting with my friends, Mr Herr Kohl, Mr Monsieur Chirac and the Prime Minister of Finland, whose name I did not catch. I made a not inconsiderably tough speech warning the others that Britain was only prepared to drive in the slow lane under severe speed restrictions and with the fast lane very definitely closed off with cones. Everyone was very impressed by my realism and agreed with the points I had made. Afterwards Mr Herr Kohl read out the official communique, which said that it was "full steam ahead to a federal superstate of Europe, run by Germany". This showed how successfully I had won the argument, but for some reason the newspapers did not seem to grasp this. They were much more interested in Mr Herr Kohl's lunch which was as follows:

10 Pigs' Stomachs, roasted in 2 kilolitres of lard

1 metric tonne of Sauerkraut mit Kartoffeln

All washed down with 300 steins of Hoffmeisterplan Lager.

As I said to my wife Norman: "It seems that Mr Kohl will eat absolutely anything." "Yes," she said, "including you for breakfast." As usual, she completely missed the point.

Sunday

Today I flew back from my historic Euro-summit meeting, to find that Mr Meyer, my press officer, was in a state of not inconsiderable excitement. "Prime Minister," he said, "we have discovered that Humphrey, the Downing Street cat, has gone missing." "I did not know we had a cat," I replied. "Oh, yes, you do," said Mr Meyer, "you are very fond of him and you are heartbroken that he has gone missing for nearly six months." Mr Meyer had apparently already told the story to all the newspapers. I thought this was all rather odd. "Was Humphrey here to catch mice?" I asked. "No, Prime Minister," he said

with a strange wink, "but he may catch us a few votes." I did not know what he was talking about, and suggested that he should go to bed to rest the strange tic in his eye.

Monday

Guess what! Humphrey, the missing cat, has been found! Mr Meyer came in to tell me this in triumphant mood. "Here is the schedule of your TV and radio appearances." "This is for me to talk about the peace process, is it?" I asked. "No," he said, "this is serious. It's for you to talk about the return of Humphrey." "Oh," I said. "What do I say?" "You say that you are relieved and delighted. Then you say 'There is another occupant of Downing Street who keeps coming back when people have written him off'." This is a very good joke which Mr Meyer says will definitely win me the next election. Not that we weren't going to win it before. Oh no.

Tuesday

Mr Meyer said this morning that he was very pleased with the cat coverage. "It made up for your failure at the Majorca Summit," he said. "But now," he said, "we've got something else for you to be delighted about. Guess who is coming to dinner with you tonight? It is Mrs Thatcher. I have already told the press that you are delighted, and you are to give her a kiss on the doorstep at 8.32 pm, just in time for the 9 o'clock News." "But I hate her," I said. "I would rather kiss the cat." "That's a great idea, Prime Minister," he said. "We will do that tomorrow. It is now time for you to get ready for your dinner opportunity."

I have to admit that in my judgement it was a very unusual dinner. At half-past-eight Mrs Thatcher arrived in her very big car, smiling and holding up a copy of her new book. Everybody took photographs of her, and then she came to the door so that I could kiss her when Mr Meyer shouted "Now!" We then went inside and Mrs Thatcher said that she unfortunately had a

prior engagement and left by the back door, pausing only to snatch up a bottle of whisky from the drinks tray. My wife Norman was in no small measure annoyed, as she had already microwaved three portions of M&S's Partytime Crab Fingers with Broccoli Bakes.

Wednesday

When I arrived in my office this morning there was a note on my desk saying, "Come in and see me at once, M.H. Check if light is green first." Luckily, the green light was on and I went straight in. Mr Heseltine seemed to have lost his desk and he was sitting on a very large gold chair in the middle of the room, with a funny crown on his head. "Ah, John," he said. "This is a terrible day for Britain. We have been humiliated in the European Courts." He then explained that we had lost some case against the IRA. "The media, of course, wanted an official government reaction from the very top, and I have given them one. I thought you ought to know what our line is." This was very helpful of Mr Heseltine, and I thanked him, but I am not sure he heard what I said, as suddenly the room filled with the sound of a huge choir singing a song about Jerusalem from The Last Night of the Proms.

Friday

All the papers are full of how angry Mr Heseltine is about this court case with the IRA, and how this time Britain is going to stand up to Europe. This will be very popular, and shows that Mr Heseltine is really trying to help me win the next election. We are so friendly in fact that he called me into his office again today, to tell me that next Monday I was going to make the whole country metric. "It is to be called M-Day, John, in your honour," he said. "So, if it is really popular, everyone will associate it with you." I asked him why we were doing it. "Is this another of those ideas from Brussels? They are very unpopular." "Oh, no," he said "Brussels *did* tell us to do it, but it was entirely your idea that we should agree to it." He then put on another song which I recognised called "Rule Britannia". Something is not quite right about all this, but I cannot put my finger on it. I went back to my office, only to find that Humphrey had knocked over all the biros on my desk and had chewed up one of my "Bastard" books.

Sunday

This week is conference week and it will be, in my judgement, the most historic week in the history of my prime ministership. At last I will reassert my authority over the party, not that I have in any way lost it, and begin the great fight back that will bring us our completely deserved triumph at the next election. Not that we were in any danger of losing it. Oh no. Since I won my great leadership victory in the summer the whole party has rallied behind me. I no longer even need any of my "Bastard" books. Every single Tory MP now has total confidence in Majorism!

No sooner had I written the above paragraph, which was entirely accurate at the time I wrote it, than my new Chairman of the Party, Mr Mawhinney, ran into the room without knocking, repeatedly shouting the word "Bastard!" in his funny Irish voice. "Have you seen the papers, John?" he shouted. "No," I replied, in my far-too-busy-preparing-my-keynote-conference-speech voice. "What's happened?" "Read this," he said, throwing down a copy of the *Observer*. Across the top of the front page was a huge headline reading "Is There Too Much Sex In The Media? — See Full Frontal Pics Inside". "That's shocking," I said. "No, underneath that, you idiot!" he screamed, reminding me in no small measure of his fellow Ulsterman Mr Paisley. "Very Top Senior Tory Minister Defects To Blair: New Blow To Major," it said. At first I was a bit worried, thinking it might be Mr Clarke or Mr Waldegrave, and we would have to find someone else to bring in the biscuits. But then I saw it was someone called Mr Howarth, whom I had never heard of. "What is the problem?" I said. "Well, if it goes on like this we may soon be forced to have an election!" he yelled. "Good," I said, "because I will win and then we will be back in power for another five years." For some reason Mr Mawhinney then began to bang his head against the wall.

Monday

Here we are in Blackpool for our historic conference. I am glad to say that no one has taken any notice of Mr Howarth. They are all wearing badges saying "Hang the Traitor". I went to a meeting organised by the Young Conservatives. It cannot have been well advertised because there was only one small boy present called Justin Squitt. However, he was a great fan of mine. He slapped me on the back and said "Can I have your job?" "Surely you mean my autograph?" I said, laughing, to show I have a sense of humour. I asked him where all the other Young Conservatives were, and he said "In the Labour Party."

At last the conference began with a tremendous speech from Mr Mawhinney. He had discovered a brilliant fact which would destroy the Labour Party forever. It was even better than the one about the Labour Council putting up the statue of a hippopotamus. This time it was about a Labour Council which was giving Asian ladies thousands of pounds to play hopscotch all day in the street. This is a real election winner and the conference rightly gave him a standing ovation.

Wednesday

When I went into the hall this morning I was glad to see a lot of people wearing badges saying "Hang the Asian Hopscotch Women". They were all looking forward to the big speech by Mr Portaloo, and we were not disappointed. His main argument was that the SAS were wonderful and therefore everyone should vote Conservative. I think this is nearly as good as Mr Mawhinney's hopscotch story.

No sooner had I written the above paragraph than I heard the bad news on the BBC. It seems that Mr Mawhinney was completely wrong and that Asian women do not play hopscotch after all. I am beginning to think that he is almost as hopeless as his predecessor Mr Hanley. I may have to start a new book for "Idiots" with Mr Mawhinney as the first entry. Everyone knows that Asian ladies cannot play hopscotch because of their long saris. Perhaps this senior Tory should join the Labour Party like the other one whose name I can't remember!

Thursday

What a good thing that Mr Heseltine had driven all the way up from Downing Street to be with us. He was in wonderful form, reading out some of the jokes he told the Conference in 1995, 1976 and 1979. He had a particularly brilliant attack on how Mr Callaghan's government sent millions of Labour rats into the street to eat the unburied corpses which lay rotting in the snow. "But then this government abolished the rats and introduced the poll tax!" he shouted, to a huge roar of laughter. "Make no mistake," he said, "my government will not go back to the bad old days when the Labour Party led a general strike and brought the country to a halt during the three-day week." As my wife Norman said afterwards: "With a leader like this, how can we lose?" I was about to thank her for being so supportive, when my mobile phone rang. It was my brother Terry to say that I must be sure to watch his new television series. "I'm at the Crazy Horse Saloon in Paris," he said. "It's nearly as funny as your Conference, although the boobs here are bigger than Mr Mawhinney's!" "I have better things to do with my time than listen to you talking about that sort of thing," I told him.

"That's not what you used to say when you were nipping over the road to Mrs Kierans," he replied. An official then came up and asked me not to use my mobile, as it was getting picked up by the sound system and relayed all over the conference hall.

Friday

Today was my turn to wow the conference. I had spent a long time writing my speech (which was written for me by Mr Morris Norris) and I was in no small measure pleased with it.

There was one particularly brilliant new idea which will help bring about my "classless society". We are going to help more people go to public school. Then we will have more men like Mr Hurd, Mr Waldegrave and Mr Blair.

The ending of my speech was, however, the very best bit of all. I used all the techniques that I have learnt from my new voice coach, Mrs Doris Morris from the Doris Morris Elocution School in Purley.

The important thing, according to Mrs Norris, is to try and sound as though you believe what you are saying. This was very helpful, as was her suggestion to bang the podium when making a particularly weak point in order to make it sound better.

Anyway, I announced that victory at the next election will mean the end of socialism. "That is because Tony Blair will get in," said my wife Norman, but luckily no one heard because there was so much applause.

Another of my favourite bits of my speech was a moving passage about my father. "This will provide a very personal touch," Mr Norris said when he wrote it.

I told the conference that I was proud of my heritage as a gnome-maker and that even if clever people sniggered it was not funny to me. This went down brilliantly with the conference. There was not a dry eye in the hall as tears streamed down everyone's cheeks and the delegates rolled in the aisles with emotion. Oh yes.

Monday

Today is a very historic week. I am in America where I have been chosen to be one of the "Top 150 Leaders of Mankind" to address the United Nations on its 50th birthday. A lot of very important people have been invited to speak with me. They include Sir Matthias Umbrellawallah, the Deputy Foreign Minister of the Cameroons; Señor Jerez di Oporto, the Portuguese Trade Minister; Mrs Gro Bag Rasmussen, the famous Norwegian Minister for Fjords; Prince Abdul Qum Danzin of the United Arab Sultanate Federation; and many others from all over the world. I spoke at 6.30 in the morning, which I was told by the UN was a very coveted slot, since it meant my speech would be carried live on prime time television all over the Pacific Rim, which is a very important part of the world. Oh yes. My speech, which lasted 90 seconds, was written by Mr Norris Morris and a team of no less than 50 of our most high-powered civil servants. The theme was "Bureaucratic Waste and Over-Manning". I think it went down very well, although unfortunately not many people had been able to get up so early in the morning to hear it. I was particularly pleased by the passage about how the UN had failed because of "weak, dithering, incompetent, indecisive leadership at the top".

Tuesday

I was woken up very early this morning by a phone call from Mr Heseltine's secretary in London. "Prime Minister," she said. "Mr Heseltine has arranged for you to come back on a later plane, so that you won't be too tired." Once again I thought how considerate Mr Heseltine is. Since he took up his new job as First Secretary and Head of the Government I have had much more time to do the really important tasks of a prime minister, such as keeping my notebooks up to date and reading the newspapers to see what silly mistakes my ministers have made.

My wife Norman and I got back to Downing Street just in time for the 10 o'clock news. Imagine my surprise when I saw Mr Heseltine sitting in my seat and pretending he was me during Prime Minister's Question Time. Unfortunately, Mr Heseltine made the elementary mistake of trying to respond to the questions without a ring-binder with all the answers in it. As I told Norinan, "he is not making a very good job of it". "Well, he is standing in for you," she said, giving one of her funny looks.

Wednesday

Today Mr Howard had to explain to the House of Commons why he would not be resigning. As usual he did this absolutely brilliantly, as he has now had a lot of practice at it. He said that the reason why so many prisoners had escaped this time was because of a Mr Lewis. "Mr Lewis is totally responsible for everything to do with the prisons," he said.

"I cannot intervene in any way, which is why I have now sacked him." This got a tremendous cheer from our side. Then Mr Straw, who is the Labour spokesman for people getting out of prison, tried to be even cleverer than Mr Howard. "I would draw to the House's attention," he said, "Section 47(b) of the Escaping from Prisons Regulations 1973, which makes it quite clear that, under Paragraph 18, sub section 5(d), Mr Howard should clearly have resigned." This was only part of Mr Straw's question, which went on for nearly an hour, by which time all the MPs had left the chamber. "They've all escaped," said Mr Howard, with a brilliant smirk, "just like one of my prisons — I mean Mr Lewis's."

Thursday

I was very not inconsiderably annoyed indeed to be woken up at 9.30 last night by my brother Terry telling me to make sure that I stayed in tonight to watch his new TV show, which is called "It's Terry-Ball!" "Don't you forget," he said, "like you did with my birthday, when you forgot to send me a card, even though you have hundreds of civil servants with nothing to do except remind you when it is someone's birthday." "Don't you realise," I told him in my of-course-Mr-Howard-shouldn't-resign voice, "that I am far too busy running the country to remember things like your birthday. For instance, I have just been in New York." "We all did that last year, John," said Terry, displaying in my judgement the kind of older-brother-knows-best superiority he used to show when telling me what colour to paint the hats on the garden ornaments, which all the sneering cleverdicks in London insist on calling gnomes, which they aren't. They are more like elves or dwarfs, if you want to call them anything, rather than garden ornaments, which is what they really are. I hope I have now made this clear and drawn a line under the whole matter of the naming of garden ornaments, which is not honestly a subject I have any time to worry about, since I have much more important things to do, like putting Terry in my "Bastard" book under T, between 'Teresa", i.e. Mrs Gorman, and that other woman who begins with T who I never mention, i.e. Mrs Thatcher.

Friday

Norman insisted on watching Terry's television programme even though I was very busy going through my briefing documents prior to my very important meeting with Mr Monsieur Chirac.

Halfway through, when Terry was looking down a big hole in the ground, I said to Norman: "It is very annoying to have such an embarrassing brother." "Oh, I don't know," she said. "I don't think Terry minds."

At the end of the programme which I did not watch (because I was far too busy reading the notes Mr Heseltine had kindly prepared for my meeting with Mr Monsieur Chirac), Terry tried to deliver a postcard to Number 10, but was quite rightly stopped at the iron gates at the end of the street. As I explained to Norman: "Mrs Thatcher did one good thing at least — putting up the gates so that Terry cannot get in with his postcard."

November

Monday

Today for once really is a very historic day because I heard on the news that the prime minister of Israel Mr Rabin had been shot. This is very sad because Mr Rabin was in the middle of a peace process. Like many world statesmen involved in peace processes, he made enemies, particularly the right wing in his own country, many of whom are clearly several apples short of a picnic.

It might have helped if Mr Rabin had kept a book of the names of all the mad people in his country who did not recognise what a great peacemaker he was. Some statesmen do this. Mr Heseltine rang through on our special direct hot line to say that I would be flying out to Israel to join all the other world statesmen at the funeral. Imagine my not inconsiderable annoyance when I boarded the aeroplane and found that I had been given a seat between Mr Blair and Mr Ashdown. Mr Blair was in the window seat and kept on saying things like, "Look, John, there's Brussels — isn't it beautiful?" Mr Ashdown meanwhile was in the aisle seat, reading a book, which kept on making him laugh out loud. When I looked closer I was in no small measure furious to see that it was Terry's book which he had bought at Smith's in the departure lounge. While we were flying over Strasbourg, which needless to say Mr Blair pointed out with one of his silly smiles which he thinks are going to win him the election, which they are not, oh no, our pilot Captain Collimore made an announcement. "Please refasten your seat belts," he said, "as we are very fortunate to have His Royal Highness the Prince of Wales at the controls." For some reason Mr Blair stopped smiling.

Tuesday

Today while Mr Rabin was being buried, I met a large number of world statesmen and had many important summit conferences, some of which lasted over 10 seconds. My friend Mr Herr Kohl said: "Guten Morgen, Herr Major, it is good to know you have left your country in ze excellent hands of Herr Heseltine. Herr Hezzler is ze vun to make ze trains run on time, nicht war?" Many of the other leaders said the same thing in their own languages, or at least I think they did. As for my own peace process, I was very pleased to meet Mr Bruton, who is the Teacuph of Ireland, who assured me that his friend Mr Adams would not be handing over even a water pistol until the British occupying forces had returned to England to be tried for murder in front of the European Court of Human Rights.

Breakfast in Israel is not at all agreeable. There are no Coco-Pops and no bacon. All they have is grapefruit segments and yoghurt, which Prince Charles told me he enjoyed very much. He was very friendly to me when we met at the service, and asked me what I did for a living and whether I had come a long way.

Wednesday

In my hotel room last night I watched the Good Morning Globe Show on the CNN channel with Waldo Applebaum and Barbara Blackadder. It was not very interesting, except for the last item which was called "Those Krazy Brits".
Apparently, while I have been away, the government has had a huge defeat on the Nolan Report. "No, we have not," I said to the television. "I commissioned the Nolan Report, and I am delighted that they have voted in favour of my idea." But then Mr Applebaum said: "Poor old Johnnie Major — goofed again! Doesn't that guy ever get anything right?" "Oh no," I told Mr Applebaum crossly, "I am in no way to blame. Mr Heseltine is in charge while I am away." Miss Blackadder, ignoring my very sensible point, then showed a photograph of a man falling into a large pile of manure. "That's how it must feel to be Prime Minister of Britain tonight. As we say, 'Sleazy come, sleazy go. Have a nice night!' " Then there was a weather map for Montreal.

Thursday

Today I flew to a place called New Zealand which is where they are having a Commonwealth Conference. It was a very long flight, but luckily when I arrived there were some real world statesmen to talk to, not just Mr Blair and Mr Ashdown crowing about how I had been defeated on Nolan, which I had not been. Oh no. It was Mr Heseltine who was defeated. Anyway, at the big dinner with the Queen, I was very privileged to sit quite near to her with Mrs Tiri Kai O'Halloran, who is the wife of the foreign minister of New Zealand, and Sir Ramprakash Saltimbokka, who is the prime minister of Sarawak. "We very much liked your television programme," he said. "The one where you went to visit the Polish gnome factory." I had to very much put him in his place for making such a silly remark. "For a start," I told him, "they are not gnomes, they are garden ornaments. And, secondly, I am not my brother Terry. I am John Major, the prime minister of Great Britain." "Then you are a complete bastard," said Sir Ramprakash suddenly. "You are a friend of the nuclear fascist Chirac. Down with nukes. Down with yourself." Mrs O'Halloran then butted in: "Yes, and you didn't even let your brother post his postcard at Number Ten Downing Street. What could be lower than that?" So saying, they both got up from the table and went to join Mr Mangoechutney, the Life President of the Democratic Dictatorship of Rumbabwe.

Friday

The Nigerians have upset everyone by hanging all their opposition. It is certainly going too far in my view, although a lot of my fellow leaders here seem to think it is a very good idea which they wish they had thought of.

Mr Heseltine rang me up this morning to tell me that I am outraged by the executions and that Britain will no longer sell the Nigerians any weapons.

"Do you mean we didn't sell any to Iraq?" I asked him. "Exactly, John," he said. "You're learning. Who knows? One day you could become deputy prime minister."

Saturday

Mr Mawhinney has sent me a fax telling me not to worry but our communications chief Mr Ken Pipe has resigned and written to all the papers saying the Conservative Party is useless.

I must admit that at first I was to some small degree concerned at this, but fortunately I soon realised that this was yet another disaster for Mr Heseltine, who has been in charge of things while I am away.

When Mr Heseltine appeared on the television today on "Good Morning Kiwi Round-Up" to announce the sanctions against Nigeria, I told him to his face: "You are hopeless" and switched him off. That is the way to deal with Mr Heseltine. Oh yes.

Sunday

Today is Remembrance Day. Luckily this is written in my diary lest I forget it. Which I didn't. I was not inconsiderably irritated therefore to turn on the television in my room and see on "Late Night Kiwi Round-Up" that Mr Heseltine was standing where I normally stand at the Cenotaph, putting down the wreath.

Anybody would think that he was Prime Minister, which he is not.

I rang him up to remind him of this and a woman told me that Mr Heseltine could not take any calls because he was too busy writing the Queen's speech for next week and simultaneously having his portrait painted in oils ready to hang in the National Portrait Gallery next to Mr Churchill's.

December

Monday

Today I have been invited to give a very historic speech at a place called the Mansion House. Everyone who is important will be there. So I have decided to explain once and for all just where I stand on Europe, i.e.we are in the fast lane but going slowly because there is a contraflow system in operation with a two-lane northbound restriction and oncoming traffic using the hard shoulder. This does not stop some people trying to overtake by driving much too fast, i.e. Mr Blair, who should, in my judgement, have his licence taken away before he wins the election, which of course he is not going to do. Oh no.

When my wife Norman and I arrived at the Mansion House I thought that perhaps Sir Robin Butler must have written down the wrong day in my Ryman's Executive Diary, because there was no one there, except a few waiters. One of them came up to us and said, "She's on now, quick or you'll miss it," and ran off towards the kitchen where there was a lady with blonde hair on the television talking about her betrayal by useless men. "I have no time for women with blonde hair going on television to talk about their betrayal by useless men," I said. "I have more important things to do, i.e. make my very important speech." Which I then did. It was very well received by everyone present, i.e.Norman, especially the bit where I took a very firm line on the Single Currency, saying we will wait and see how things turn out.

Tuesday

I was very not inconsiderably annoyed this morning to see that my historic speech had been given no mention at all in any of the newspapers. Instead, all they seemed to be interested in is that woman on TV last night who turns out to be Princess Diana talking about her problems. I even recieved a summons from the

TRUMP

Palace where the Queen wanted to see me urgently. "Did you see it?" were her opening words. She then continued shouting: "What on earth are we going to do with her? I suppose there is only one thing for it. We'll have to give her what she wants and make her an ambassador."

"Whatever you say, ma'am," I replied, giving the benefit of all my experience as an elder statesman.

"I have written down a list of places where she could be ambassador on a full-time basis." The Queen then handed over a piece of paper on which was written: 1. Ulan Bator; 2. South Georgia; 3. Muroroa Atoll; 4. The Moon. "But surely," I said, thinking quickly on my feet and without the benefit of my *Daily Telegraph* Map of the World, "all those places are rather far away, and some of them are a bit dangerous?" "Good grief," said the Queen, "and we thought Diana was thick..."

This matter is obviously preying on Her Majesty's mind. "We all have relatives we are ashamed of who go on TV and make fools of themselves," I told her reassuringly.

Wednesday

My friend Mr Clinton rang up this morning in a state of great excitement, as I gathered when he shouted down the telephone "Yabba dabba doo!" "Yes, Mr President?" I enquired. "Great noos, John, yes sirree," he said. "I've sure sorted the Bosnonian problem. I've kicked ass and cracked heads together and it's peace in our time, baby, thanks to yours truly." "That is certainly good news," I told him. "And now it's your turn, John," he went on, "I've agreed to send in 13,000 of your British troops to keep my new peace." "But we haven't got 13,000 troops," I said. "Sure you have, Johnny," he said, "you're pulling them out of Ulster, thanks to my next peace process, when I make my friend Gerry Adams President of All-Ireland. Before I could reply that it wasn't that simple, Mr Clinton had rung off and there was only a tape of a saxophone playing.

Thursday

I am getting really in no small measure angry with Mr Blair. Today he announced that he would be cutting taxes. What a pathetic idea! He will do anything to win the election. At our Cabinet meeting this morning, everyone urged Mr Clarke to cut taxes at once, saying that it was the only way to win the election. "Oh no," I said, "we are not going to resort to cheap tricks like that. We should fight on my record." There was a long silence, and then Mr Clarke said that perhaps he would go for the cheap trick after all.

Friday

Dr Mawhinney came in to give me my list of appointments for the day. One of them was to ring up a Mr Bashir at the BBC to ask if he would interview me on *Panorama* to put my side of the story to the nation. When I rang up a very nice lady's voice said: "You are in a queue. Just hold the line," and then they played that very famous tune called The Four Seasons, which Norman plays on CD while we eat our supper. Eventually I was put through to a Miss Researcher who told me that I could not go on their programme, because they were already doing an in-depth documentary about my brother Terry. I hope he does not try to post a Christmas card to 10 Downing Street, otherwise I will have him arrested for treason. Oh yes.

Saturday

Today really is an incredibly historic day. It is five years to the day since I replaced Mrs Thatcher. I have decided to commemorate this event by buying a new book from Ryman's in which to list all my achievements. So far I have put in:

- The Cones Hotline.
- The provision of more toilets on the motorways.
- The Citizen's Charter and associated Chartermarks.
- The award of a CBE to Cyril Washbrook, the famous England cricketer.
- Being on *Desert Island Discs* with Sue Lawley.
- Stopping Terry coming in to Number Ten to deliver his postcard.

I have now served longer than any British Prime Minister apart from Francis Urquhart. But as I explained to my wife Norman, he is not a real person.

"Does that exclude you, then?" she asked, once again failing to see the point. There are times in this job when you really feel like resigning. As I told the very nice man from the *Daily Telegraph*, there have been two occasions when I nearly packed the whole thing in.

"Third time lucky," Norman said.

Sunday

In the middle of the night I suddenly thought of another achievement to put in my notebook. The Peace Process.

Monday

Imagine my irritation when President Clinton rang me very early in the morning indeed, i.e. 4 a.m.

"I've had a lot of hassle getting through to you, John. When I asked to speak to the Prime Minister they kept giving me some guy called Hesselstone."

"What do you want?" I asked in my no-nonsense-four-o'clock-in-the-morning voice.

"I'm coming over to do the photo-shoot for my Irish peace process. I want you and Gerry Adams shaking hands with me in the middle. By Thursday. Gottit?"

Once again he rang off and left me listening to a song about when Irish eyes are smiling which ended with the words "Vote Democrat. Vote O'Clinton."

Tuesday

At last I think we have turned the corner! Not that we needed to turn the corner, oh no. But undoubtedly Mr Clarke's very clever budget has put us on track for a historic victory at the next election. First he fooled everyone into thinking that he was going to announce huge tax cuts to make us popular. Then he did nothing of the sort! This completely wrong-footed the Labour Party who were left speechless at his cleverness. When he had finished there was complete silence and then one or two Labour MPs shouted "bye, bye". This was obviously their way of saying that Mr Blair was on his way out, since he had no answer to Mr Clarke's brilliant proposal to increase the upper limit of capital gains allowances by £1.57 a week for everyone in Tax Band G. Our side was so impressed that they all rushed out to the bar to buy the new cheap whisky which, thanks to Mr Clarke, now costs only £12.58 a bottle. When I got home, my wife Norman had done a calculation showing that a married couple with grown-up children, living in 10 Downing Street, would soon have to move house.

Wednesday

I am very not inconsiderably seriously in no small measure furious at Mr Clinton. Instead of the papers being full of Mr Clarke's brilliant budget, they were full of Mr Clinton's visit to Belfast. They all said that it was Mr Clinton who had brought peace to Ireland, when it is extremely well-known that only one person has brought peace to Ireland, i.e. me and Mr Bruton (although Mr Bruton has not done very much). It wasn't Mr Clinton who had the brilliant idea of having a twin-track peace process, which works like a dual-carriageway, with a central reservation for safety purposes keeping apart the two sides who are going in opposite directions. It was me, and it is really in my judgement not inconsiderably infuriating to see him going to Ireland just to win votes for his next election. If anyone deserves to win an election because of bringing peace to Northern Ireland, it is me.

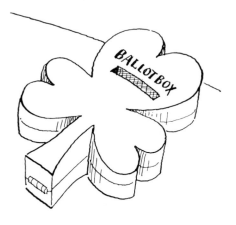

Thursday

Mr Rifkind came in very excitedly to say that France was collapsing in chaos. There were millions of people on strike, rubbish was piling up in the streets and bodies were remaining unburied. "Thank goodness," he said in his funny Scottish dalek voice, "that terrible things like that couldn't happen here any longer." "You are right," I said. "Thanks to my brilliant negotiating of the opt-out clause on the social chapter at Maastricht." "Not entirely," said Mr Rifkind. "I was thinking more of Mrs Thatcher's brilliant and historic success in abolishing the trade unions." "Don't I get any credit?" I asked him not uncrossly. "Of course," he said. "Since you have abolished all the public services, they cannot grind to a halt."

Friday

Today I was in Florence which is in Italy to meet the Italian prime minister. "Hullo, Mr Signor Andreotti," I said to the small fat man who came to meet me at the airport. "No,

he is in prison," said
the Italian. "Oh yes," I
said. "You are Mr
Signor Berlusconi."
"No," he said, "he is in
prison too. I am
Lamberto Dini." "Ah," I
said, "so you are the
one who will be in
prison next week." At
this he looked not
inconsiderably cross, so
our meeting did not get
off to the best of starts.

This was a pity since we had very important matters to
discuss, ie how to stop Mr Herr Kohl and Mr Monsieur Chirac
telling us what to do. I could tell that Signor Dini was very
keen to get into the fast lane towards the Monetary Union.
But unfortunately his battery was flat and someone had
stolen the wheels to his car. Britain, on the other hand, has a
very good car with plenty of wheels and a battery that is in
perfect working order, thanks to the fact that we left the
ERM by a slip-road. So now obviously Britain is not so keen
to get back in the fast lane and have big German cars coming
up behind us flashing their lights. I explained all this in
detail to Mr Dini, who listened very carefully and then said:
"If I was you, Giovanni, I would no more eata the beef."

Saturday

I am heartily in no small measure sick of reading stories
suggesting that I am going to resign and that Mr Heseltine is
going to take over. In fact I went in to see Mr Heseltine, who
let me in after only half an hour's waiting by the door with
the red light on, and told him what I thought.

"If these sort of unfounded rumours persist," I said, "I shall
have to resign."

Mr Heseltine smiled in agreement and then joked that in
that case he would take over, as agreed. He is a very kind
man with a wonderful sense of humour that is not always
appreciated.

Sunday

Once again I am pleased to record that Downing Street
security is second to none. The police rang to say that there
was a gentleman at the gate claiming to be my brother and

attempting to deliver a Christmas card in order to save the 25p stamp. I told them to employ a simple test on the intruder, viz: "Ask him what colour hats the fishing gnomes wore in the 'D' batches of January 1953."

This was a trick question, as the gnomes made for Wallington Garden Centres that year did not wear hats at all!

The police said that the impostor had given the correct answer, adding that it was all in his book on page 168 as I knew perfectly well even though I said I had not read it.

I suggested that the police hold the suspect over night anyway to teach him a lesson.

Monday

I am not inconsiderably very annoyed by my friend Sir David Lightbulb, who has let me down very badly by dying. This is really very inconsiderate of him, as it means that my majority has been reduced to three, if we lose the by-election. Which of course we won't. But we might, because he only had a majority of 16,000, which is not enough these days. Dr Mawhinney even suggested that we should get ready for a general election. What rubbish, I told Dr Mawhinney. "Of course we don't want a general election yet, because I still have so much of my programme to complete." Dr Mawhinney in his rather rude way asked me what I had in mind. "Er," I said, "well, there is my plan to give chartermarks to nursery schools... er... free vouchers for cone-lines... er... all right, let's have a general election. I'll just go and ask Mr Heseltine which days he is free."

Tuesday

Today I flew to Madrid with Mr Clarke for another very important Euro-summit. Unfortunately, it took several hours to find our hotel which was on the outskirts of the city next to a new fish processing plant which was called "Los Pesces Di Cornwallo". The hotel only had one room plus shower which Mr Clarke and I had to share. When we got there, our landlady Mrs Portillo gave us a large, gold-edged invitation from Mr Herr Kohl and Mr President Chirac, to visit them at their hotel which was called The El Magnifico. They are very obviously very lucky to have been given very nice rooms in the same building as the conference. When we got there on the tram, the drawing room of Mr Kohl's penthouse suite was even larger than Mr Heseltine's office. Mr Kohl had put towels on all the chairs, so we had to stand up while he told us what we were all going to agree to the next day.

"Remember, mein kleine freund," he said, "ein volk, ein Reich, ein currency." I had to speak to him very sternly in my special standing-up-to-Europe voice. "Although I have neither ruled out nor ruled in any British participation in the single currency," I said, "I have however prepared some possible names for it in this special book from Ryman's." I then read out my suggestions which were:

- the shilling
- the half-crown
- the ten-shilling note

and my favourite, which I left till last,

- the Major.

Mr Kohl took my list and after considering it very carefully he threw my book in the bin.

"It has already been decided," he said. "It will be called the Euro." "Oh," I said, "that is a very interesting idea, but thanks to my Maastricht opt-out I am reserving my position with regard to this one." "Get out," he said, in his friendly way, "Jacques Chirac and I have got work to do." Mr Clarke and I missed the last tram back, and it was 3 o'clock in the morning by the time we got back to our hotel.

Wednesday

Today was a very historic day, when it was finally decided what the new name of the European currency is going to be. The voting was as follows: for the name Euro, 14 countries. Other suggestions (eg, florin, emu, pound, etc), 1 vote, i.e. me. Mr Clarke whispered, "It's just like the Eurovision Song Contest except without Terry." "What has my brother got to do with it?" I said to him crossly. "I would be obliged if you would not try to distract me by talking about television personalities who are of no historical importance at all, unlike their brothers who are about to make a very

important speech." I then told all the other delegates that in my judgement the European currency was a completely mad idea, which would not work and would lead to the end of civilisation. Everyone was very shocked by how outspoken I was, and after a long silence Mr Herr Kohl shouted down from the top of the table

EUREAU de CH

"So, you are against it then?" "On the contrary," I replied. "I have not yet made up my mind." That certainly shut them up, and they all immediately began to laugh.

Thursday

I was very in no small measure excited to be rung up by Mr Moore, the Editor of the *Daily Telegraph*, who said that he was so impressed by my attack on the single currency at Madrid that he wanted me to write an article about it for his newspaper. "When is the deadline?" I said. "Don't worry about that," he said, "we got Dr Mawhinney to write it, and we're running it tomorrow under the headline 'Why I Say EMU Stinks by Prime Minister John Major'."

Friday

I am even more not inconsiderably annoyed than usual with my ex-friend Mr Ashby-De-La-Louche. He has let me down even more badly than Sir David Lightbulb.

Mr Ashby has not even had the decency to die unexpectedly but has been made bankrupt by bringing a silly libel action about whether or not he sleeps with other men.

Dr Mawhinney tells me that this is terrible news since it will cut our majority down to two, since bankrupts cannot remain Members of Parliament.

"This is a very sleazy and unpleasant business which reflects badly on the party," I said.

"Yes," said Dr Mawhinney. "Why don't we bung Ashby a load of money to save his seat and keep our majority?"

"Good idea," I agreed.

Christmas Day

We had a very nice day at Chequers and I was given some very nice Christmas presents including:

● Some chocolate Euros from Mr Herr Kohl wrapped up in gold paper with his face on them.

● A Ryman's Whistling Key-Ring from Mr Ryman himself with a card that said "To one of our most valued customers."

● A gold watch from Mr Heseltine engraved to "J.M. from P.M., wishing you well in your retirement."

This year I did not get a present from my brother Terry due to an unfortunate mistake which occurred with the security men in Downing Street. They told me there was a suspicious package from someone calling himself "Terry".

I told them not to take any chances, as "Terry" could easily be short for "terrorist". They then blew it up in a controlled explosion.

However, all that was discovered in the package were two pairs of grey socks from Sockworld of Croydon (formerly J.R. Ballard, Gentlemen's Hosiery) and a printed card saying, "Happy Holiday, from your brother, TV's Terry Major Ball."

New Year's Eve

"Ring out the old, ring in the new," I said to my wife Norman as the clock struck 9. "Oh good," she said, "shall I start packing then?" — missing the point as usual. "Oh no," I told her, "this New Year marks a new start, new beginnings, new initiatives, new policies..." "...and New Labour" she added, missing the point for the second time in a matter of minutes. I poured myself another glass of Dom Portillo's Very Dry British Sherry to toast the future. "The Party," I said, "is now firmly on track for my fifth election victory in a row. We are a broad church, driving at a prudent speed down the middle lane, in accordance with the new EU directive on Coaches on Motorways. And above all, thanks to my heroic victory over Mr Redwood, our Party is now totally united."

SEKONDMENT

January 1996

New Year's Day

As I said, we are totally united, except for someone called Emma Nicholson, who has decided that she is going to join the Liberal Democrats because the government is too right wing. Fortunately, Mr Heseltine managed to get on all the breakfast TV and radio programmes and he was very statesmanlike indeed. He said that he was not going to indulge in personal abuse about a useless old cow like Miss Nicholson, who had only committed her unprincipled act of treason because he hadn't given her a job.

Then Mr Portaloo came on to say that it was nonsense that the government was too right wing. "It is not nearly right wing enough," he said. "It is high time that certain other people at the highest levels of the Party joined the Liberal Democrats, so that we can have a real Conservative government which cracks down on benefit scroungers, foreigners and Europhiles."

Wednesday

Dr Mawhinney has been doing his sums and he has worked out that we only have a majority of one. "Then we'd better have an election," I told him. His face went not inconsiderably white and he said: "But then we wouldn't have a majority at all, prime minister." We therefore decided to do the honourable thing and hang on to power for as long as possible.

Thursday

I have made it perfectly clear that I will make no deals of any kind with the Ulster Unionists, just because I need their votes to hang on to power for as long as possible. In order to leave no possible misunderstanding about my very firm position on this, I invited Mr Trimble and Dr Paisley to a special seven-course banquet at Number 10, with a musical accompaniment provided by the Fife And Drum Marching Band of the 9th Apprentice Boys Orange Order, who are to receive a £2 million grant, I hear, from the National Lottery.

Friday

I had a very nice note from Dr Paisley thanking me for my hospitality and saying that in return he would not hesitate to bring down the government unless I arrested Mr Adams and put him on trial for high treason. I replied that I would give very careful consideration to his constructive proposals. The main thing is not to endanger my peace process, which has been my main achievement in government so far, even more historic than the Cones Hotline, the Citizen's Charter and the opt-out from the Social Chapter in the Maastricht Treaty. The peace process is still going extremely well. Today there were only six murders in Northern Ireland, by a group called the Irish Republican Force for Direct Action Against John Major, who clearly are not related in any way to the IRA or Mr Adams.

Saturday

I was very pleased to see from the breakfast television that another of my policies is working extremely well — i.e. the privatisation of water. There were wonderful pictures of people in the north of England having water delivered to their doors by special lorries provided by the efficient new water companies. All people have to do is stand outside their houses with old kettles, jugs and baby baths and they can have almost as much water as they want — and all free! This would not have happened in the bad old days of the nationalised water boards, with their old-fashioned tap system.

Sunday

My friend Sir David Frost has invited me *again* on to his influential Sunday morning television programme *No One's Watching*.

A researcher rang me up ten minutes before the broadcast began, saying that Mr Blair was out of the country and Mr Heseltine was too busy running it — so could I get in a taxi and come on over?

I did do at once, stopping only to shout at my brother Terry who was still waiting by the security gates to give me my Christmas card. "You're not the only one who goes on television, you know!" I shouted. "Oh no."

The abrasive Sir David tried to catch me out as usual by asking me to fill in as much time as I could before "Power Rangers" by saying whatever I liked.

I seized the opportunity to, spell out my message to the party in no uncertain terms.

"We are in the centre lane slightly to the right and it would be madness now for us to hand over the controls to an airline pilot who does not even know how to fly a rubber dinghy in the Serpentine. Oh yes or, rather, no!"

I also made a veiled attack on Mr Portaloo to show that I am firmly *not* in the right lane, as I previously said.

"Michael is a great patriot but, looking back at his conference speech about the SAS, he would be the first to admit that he made a complete fool of himself."

I ended by saying that unless the party stopped its bickering and mud-slinging then all those useless bastards would lose us the election.

Mr Frost was very impressed and said in a firm voice: "And now over to Linda Zimbabwe with this morning's weather."

Monday

Today was a very historic day indeed, when I went to Paris, which is in France, for the funeral of Mr Monsieur Mitterrand. Although I cannot say I knew him well, I was a close personal friend and therefore I was placed in a position of great honour in Row 78B (restricted view). I was next to many world statesmen, including Mr Vaclav Bratpak, the Foreign Minister of Slavonia, Life President Gonzo of French Limpopoland (formerly French Rhumbabwe), and His Imperial Majesty King Babar the Elephant of Celesteville. When I looked round the pillar I could just see, in the distance, the unmistakable figure of my friend Mr Herr Kohl,

sitting in the front
row next to Mr
Mitterrand's dog.
I was very moved to
see tears rolling down
Mr Kohl's cheeks at
the loss of his old
friend. Should I cry as
well, I wondered.
I decided that this
would give the wrong
signals to our Euro-
sceptics. But it would
be quite wrong of me
to encourage them by
smiling. Oh no.
I decided that the

prudent course was to take the middle way by neither crying
nor smiling, but looking not inconsiderably solemn.

Tuesday

I am entirely uninterested in Mrs Thatcher's big speech
today. No one in the government is even going to it, except
Mr Portaloo, Mr Lilley and Mr Redwood. These three are all
Bastards and are all in my Bastard book underlined in red
ink, and Mr Redwood is not even in my government at all,
owing to the fact that he resigned to try and get my job,
although he only got 89 votes, which is hardly any,
considering that no one had even heard of him.

Wednesday

All the papers have got it completely wrong, as usual. They
say that Mrs Thatcher's speech was a tremendous attack on
me. It was no such thing. When she talked about "weak,
hopeless leadership, which would lose the next election," she
was clearly referring to Mr Blair and his so-called New
Conservative Party. I am also very confused by Mrs
Thatcher's remark about a "One nation party" being a "No
nation party". Perhaps she meant a "No Asian party" like Mr
Enoch Powell wanted. Or possibly a "One Asian party",
meaning Mr Asil Nadir, who was so generous to us at the last
election. She could however have meant to say that we were a
"No station party", thereby endorsing our policy of selling off
the railways to bus companies, so they can close all the
stations down. I asked my wife Norman what she thought

Mrs Thatcher meant. She replied: "She should have said that you are a One-Notion party, since your only idea seems to be to stay in power as long as possible without doing anything."

Thursday

Who says that I am finished, apart from everyone? Today my majority went up by no less than 20 per cent, i.e. one seat. This is because I decided to let Sir Richard Body back into the Conservative Party. I therefore removed him from my "Looneys" book, where he was listed under "Picnic, apples short of a" and also "White coats, flapping of". He has pledged to give me his total and unswerving support, provided that I do whatever he says on the subject of fish. I told him I would do everything in my power to look into the fish that he was worried about. He said that this wasn't good enough and walked out. I have had to put him back into Looney book under the new heading "Extremely Fishy".

Friday

In the House of Commons today someone on the Labour side asked me if there was "a plot to get rid of me as leader". Mr Heseltine immediately jumped to his feet and said: "Yes, of course there isn't!"

Everyone laughed, including me. I laughed a great deal to prove that we are the party of laughter. Oh yes.

The other side merely repeated the question, proving that they have no new ideas.

"Are the men in grey suits going to come and get you?" they shouted. "No," I said, quick as a flash. "How can they do that when I am wearing a grey suit myself!"

This put a stop to their silly questions about a so-called plot and they were reduced to cheering loudly and singing "Goodby-eee!"

Saturday

My ex-friend Norma Lamont has finally found a seat in a town with a local branch of Thresher's. It is in Harrogate, which Mr Mawhinney tells me is a safe seat.

"He has a majority of 20,000," he told me. "Good," I said. "Then he will lose."

February

Sunday

At last, as I have been saying all along, we are certain to win the next election! Labour has made the most monumental blunder in the whole history of politics. The way ahead is now clear for me to win my record fifth election victory in a row. The incredible scandal which has gripped everyone in the nation involved one of Mr Blair's very closest friends, a lady MP called Mrs Harman, who, believe it or not, has sent her son to a grammar school. "Good for her," said my wife Norman. "He will have a good start in life, like you did. He might even end up being prime minister, especially as he is Labour." As usual, she completely missed the point.

Monday

Today I totally trounced Mr Blair in the House of Commons. Even the *Daily Mail*, which is normally a Labour paper, said that I was brilliant and that the Labour Party was finished. At Question Time he asked me about the timetable for railway privatisation, and quick as a flash I replied: "Why is Mrs Harman sending her son to a grammar school?" Our side stood up and cheered for 10 minutes. Everyone agreed that it was my finest ever performance in Parliament. We really are merciless in our attacks on Mr Blair! Mr Heseltine in his daily appearance with Mr Humphrys on the Today programme said that Mr Blair was "the criminals' friend". "Just like you and Mr Asil Nadir," said Norman, as usual being unhelpful. "No," I said. "The statistics show that crime under my government has fallen. That means that anyone who is against my government is a friend of the criminals." It is lucky I went to a grammar school, like Mrs Harman's son, so I can understand these simple logical points!

Tuesday

I'm afraid that Mr Clinton's friend, Mr Senator Mitchell, has completely failed to understand the problems of Northern Ireland. He has said that it is perfectly all right for Mr Gerry Adams to take over Northern Ireland without having to give up his weapons and that talks about this should go ahead at once. I have come up with a brilliant compromise idea which will keep the peace process going. "We will have an election," I told the Cabinet. They all went white, until I explained that I didn't mean *here* but in Northern Ireland. "I thought we were meant to have the talks first, then the election," said Mr Rifkind. "I have decided to change the order around," I explained. "So what will the talks be about?" asked Mr Waldegrave. "Having another election," I said. "We will have elections, talks, more elections, more talks — in that way we will be able to keep my peace process going indefinitely."

Wednesday

Mr Adams does not like my idea because he thinks that he will not get many votes. Mr Bruton does not like my idea either, because he thinks that if Mr Adams doesn't get many votes he won't either in his elections. Mr Clinton has also come out against my idea because if the other two don't get many votes, then there won't be many for him in *his* election, which was the only point of the peace process anyway. Thank goodness I don't have to worry about winning my election because, thanks to Mrs Harman sending her son to a grammar school, I have already won.

Thursday

Not inconsiderably terrific news from Hemsworth, where there has been a by-election! We have confounded the sceptics and retained our deposit.

What is even better, the Labour Party has been split by Mr Scargill's New Labour Party. Labour got only 16,000 votes — *well* down on the projected 16,100. And Mr Scargill got 2,000 votes — well up on the projected 3,000!

As Mr Mawhinney said, it was certainly a great day for us. He told me that Conservative MPs are now so confident that we will win the next election that 52 of them are leaving on the grounds that I can win perfectly well without them. Oh yes.

Meanwhile I am in no small measure annoyed with Mr Herr Kohl who has criticised me for going too slowly in the fast lane while he is coming up behind me in his BMW flashing his lights and shouting: "For you, English Johnny, ze European Union is over!"

He even said that unless we all unite in a Federal Europe there will be war.

"Will you be flying to Munich to see him?" asked my wife Norman, showing very little knowledge of German geography.

"The capital of Germany is Brussels," I told her, "as everyone knows. That is where Mr Herr Kohl lives with his friend Mr Monsieur Mitterrand who is dead."

"He is not the only one," she said as we ate our Marks & Spencer Balti House Executive Cucumber Soup in front of the television news.

Friday

I am glad to say that my peace process continues on its twin tracks — ie, we will have elections and then we will have talks. Or the other way round. Let there be no doubt I am flexible on this one. Only this evening Mrs R, the secret head of MI5 (Mrs Rimington) came in personally to assure me that the IRA ceasefire is holding strongly. This is very encouraging. While she was explaining this there was a very loud bang. A few seconds later Mr Mawhinney rushed in, looking white-faced, and said: "Prime Minister, your peace process has just gone up in smoke — as has the *Daily Telegraph*." "That is appalling," I said. "Has it done a lot of damage?" "Yes," he said, "it could have destroyed the only thing you've achieved in five years."

Saturday

I was in no small measure surprised to hear Mr Gerry Adams telling Mr Humphrys on the BBC that the only person responsible for the bombing was me. I immediately rang up the police to give them my alibi — ie, that I was with a Mrs R at the time the bomb went off and she would support me, although she could not be identified for security reasons. The young constable who took my call said "That's very interesting, sir. Have you tried our counselling hotline for people whose wits have been deranged by the bomb?" It just goes to show how little Mr Adams knows about anything. Everyone says that it was the IRA who let off that bomb and not me at all. I am beginning to think that Mr Adams is someone who can't be trusted.

Sunday

All the Sunday papers are saying that my peace process is at an end. They are wrong, as usual. It is my peace process, and the only person who can decide that it is at an end is me, not the IRA, who cannot stop the peace process just by letting off a few bombs and killing people. One thing is certain. I will not be talking to Mr Adams again for a not inconsiderable period of time. I rang him up at once to tell him this.

But the person I have real argument with is Mr Bruton who has accused me of throwing petrol on the flames. I had to ring the Irish police with my alibi. The young gardai who took my call said: "Yes, sor, that's very interesting. Would you care to be connected with our counselling service, Father O'Semtex?" "No," I told him, "I have much more important matters to attend to, such as putting your prime minister in my new 'Peace Bastards Book'."

These are the names so far in my book:

1. Mr Adams, who says he has not even heard of the IRA.
2. Mrs Rimington, who does not know when the IRA are going to let off their bombs.
3. Mr Bruton, who does not like my elections' plan.
4. Mr Spring, ditto.
5. Mr Clinton, who has refused to say he is sorry for talking to Mr Adams.

I am not going to talk to any of these people again.

Monday

When I showed Mr Sir Patrick Mayhew my list of people we cannot talk to any more he said: "Prime Minister, if you don't talk to any of these people then we don't have a peace process." He is not as stupid as he looks. "Well, I'm certainly not talking to Mr Adams," I said. "The only reason I originally agreed to talk to him was that he represented the IRA. But now he says that they are nothing to do with him. So there is no point in talking to him." "But he's lying," said Sir Patrick, "so you should still talk to him." "No, I will not," I said, "and I shall ring him up again to tell him so." "But we've got to talk to someone," he repeated, "or there will be no peace process at all. What about Mr Bruton?"

Tuesday

Yes, my peace process is firmly back on course again. Not that it has ever been off course, oh no. Mr Bruton and I have agreed to sign a full peace treaty covering all the main points, ie:

1. The peace process will continue.
2. Both governments are firmly committed to the peace process.
3. We shall have elections or talks or both or neither, according to whatever circumstances shall prevail at the time.

This agreement shall be known as the Proximate Declaration and will be signed by all the key parties, i.e. Mr Bruton and myself, but not Mr Adams, the IRA, the UVF, Mr Paisley, Mr Trimble or anyone in Northern Ireland.

Wednesday

Another bomb has gone off in London. But let one thing be clear. The Peace Process is continuing.

Thursday

Now that I have sorted out the Irish problem, there is only one more obstacle remaining before I win the next election. This is Mr Sir Lord Scott's Report on the arms to Iraq affair. I was slightly concerned that Mr Lord Scott might come to the conclusion that the government had behaved badly and then lied about it. I was not worried so much for myself, since I had explained to Mr Scott that, whatever I might have been told at the time, I was too busy to remember it because I was the Foreign Secretary. But I was worried for my friend Mr Waldegrave, who had clearly lied and might have to resign. I was also worried about someone called Mr Lyell, who had apparently tried to put some men in prison although they had not done anything. Obviously the most important thing was to make sure that no one had a chance to read the report before we could tell everyone what was in it. The only person we allowed to see the report was Mr Cook, who we put in a darkened room under armed guard and took away his spectacles. We gave him five minutes to read the 10,000 pages and then my friend Mr Lang stood up in the House of Commons and said that Mr Cook was a disgrace and should resign for misleading the House.

"Wasn't that us?" I whispered to Mr Lang when he sat down. "Shut up and keep laughing," said Mr Heseltine. "Then people will think you know what's going on."

Luckily it didn't matter, as Mr Lord Justice Scott had done a brilliant job, concluding that, although we might have cheated and lied, we did not mean to.

This certainly put the Labour Party on the spot and all Mr Cook could do was go pathetically through the report reading out the bits where Mr Scott had said that we had sold guns to Iraq, misled the House about it, and then tried to cover it up by putting innocent men in gaol. It was a sad sight, and the Labour MPs were reduced to shouting "Resign! Resign!" But I am afraid it is going to take much more than this to get Mr Cook to do the decent thing.

Friday

Mr Mawhinney came in with some terrible news. "One of our men has resigned!" "But Mr Scott let them off," I told him. "That was the whole point."

Mr Mawhinney then explained that it was not Mr Waldegrave or Mr Lyell but someone called Mr Thurdham. He is an MP and the third man to resign from my party, except that one of the others was a woman, viz Emma Nicholson.

Saturday

Since my majority is now down to one (owing to circumstances out of my control, i.e. so many people resigning from my party because they think I am useless, which of course I am not, oh no! it is obviously very important that I keep Mr Thurdman on my side. I therefore invited him to tea to discuss his political future.

Sunday

My tea party with Mr Thurdman was not a success. I was somewhat surprised with his wife Mrs Thurdman, who seemed to be very cross and started shouting at me. "How dare you treat Peter like this, after he has voted for you so loyally all these years!" she screamed. "Let us be calm about this," I said in my special soothing-bad-tempered-wives voice that I have had on occasion to use even in my own home! "Would you like one of these delicious peerages — I mean biscuits?" I asked, dropping a rather subtle hint. "But I thought in your new, classless society, you didn't give biscuits for political services?" Mr Thurdman replied. "We do not, Lord Thurdman," I countered. "But I have so admired your decision to vote for me in the Scott debate tomorrow that I am going to make an exception in your case, and give you this biscuit." Unfortunately, his wife interrupted at this point, shouting: "You cannot fob off my Peter with a mere biscuit! He deserves a peerage at the very least."

Monday

Today was a very historic day, perhaps surpassing all other days in its historicness. Everyone said I was finished. But, oh no. I not only survived but I have won a complete and total victory over all the other parties combined. This was the historic score, which I shall never forget:

J. Major's Team...320

The Rest of the World...319.

Winner J. Major, as per usual! A line has now been drawn under the Scott Report and everyone accepts that none of us did anything wrong, except perhaps Mr Waldegrave. We did not sell arms to Iraq, and if we did, we did not know we were doing. We did not try to send innocent men to prison, and if we did, we did it in good faith. All my friend Mr Lang had to do was keep repeating this in the debate, and poor Mr Cook was completely speechless. All he could do was make a long, dull speech, listing all the lies we had told and trying to pretend we had meant to tell them. Everyone was very bored with this and cheered wildly at the end with relief that he had finished.

Fortunately, the debate made no difference at all to the vote which was a complete triumph, as I may already have mentioned.

Let one thing be clear! I won this vote fair and square on the issue of Mr Scott saying that we only lied in good faith. Whatever the lefties at the BBC and *Telegraph* are saying, I did not have to do any deals with anyone, including Mr Thurdman, Mr Allason or Mr Paisley, whose three votes coincidentally secured my victory. Even Mrs Thatcher agreed that I had done nothing wrong, which shows that we must have been right. I might change my mind and mention her in my diary just this once.

March

Tuesday

Following my Scott triumph, my other main policy, i.e. my peace process, is also firmly back on track. Not that it has ever been off track, oh no. This morning Mr Bruton and I had a historic telephone conversation in which we agreed the following:

1. We will not be bombed to the conference table.

2. We must get to the conference table as soon as possible.

3. We have set a date for the conference of 24 May.

4. We hope this will now persuade the IRA to stop the bombing.

I have now drawn a line under the bombing.

This will be the agenda for the historic talks:

1. Proximity talks to determine the nature of the talks.

2. These will be preceded by elections which will also have to be preceded by talks about the nature of the elections.

3. These will be preceded by a referendum on whether there should be talks before the elections or after.

Wednesday

Today I am at a special conference in a place called the Pacific Rim. I am here to meet the leaders of all the countries called "Tiger Economies" because they are very frightening.

They do not of course frighten me! Oh no. I suggested to Mr Rifkind that I might even bring up the subjects of Human Rights with the Chinese delegate, who is called Mr Fuk Yu Rop. Mr Rifkind said that this was perhaps not such a good idea because it was considered bad manners in the East to mention this sort of issue.

"The thing to do," he said, "is to concentrate on trade links. That will really show them that you mean business."

Thursday

I decided to take Mr Rifkind's advice and had my photo taken shaking hands with the Chinese man. We all wore very nice shirts, incidentally, made from silk and given to us free!

"Very smooth, very cool," I said to the kind organiser who gave me a grey silk one. "Like your Mr Blair!" he replied, obviously missing the point due to his poor command of English.

Friday

Now I am in Hong Kong, staying with my old friend Chris Patten.

Mr Patten explained to me his new idea, which is to allow 2 million Chinese people to come and have a holiday in Britain, but not to stay because no one in their right mind would want to live here. It all sounded very convincing. "Do *you* have a work permit?" I asked him jokily. "I have a job lined up already," he replied. "The present occupant will shortly be retiring because he is no good and I am going to step into his shoes."

I did not really understand this and am worried that Mr Patten may have been out in the midday sun for too long.

Saturday

Next week the historic process begins with talks at Stormont. And the good news is that all the parties have agreed to come except Sinn Fein and some of the Unionists. The two sides have at last agreed on something, i.e. they are going to stay away. This is real progress.

Sunday

I stayed up all night to watch the World Cup cricket on our new Sky dish which was kindly provided by Mrs Thatcher's friend Mr Murdoch as a peace offering for the fact that his newspapers all support Mr Blair. England was playing the Pitcairn Islands, I think. This was the score:

England 27 (Christian F. 6-7, Christian-Umbrellawallah 2-3, the Rev Christian-Soldiaz 2-1).

Pitcairn Island 506-2 in 50 overs (Christian F. 166, Christian-Umbrellawallah 212, the Rev Christian-Soldiaz 112*).

This was in no small measure a creditable performance by the Pitcairners, especially as there are only 3 people on their island who play cricket. Of course, the tabloid press, such as the *Daily Telegraph*, are saying that England is in a mess and

that our captain should
resign at once and give
way to Mr Clarke or Mr
Heseltine. What
rubbish! The only
person who could
possibly lead England is
my friend Chris Patten,
and only then after I
have retired, by which
time he will be 85,
which in my view
disqualifies him from
playing cricket at any
level. I'm afraid, after
staying up so late, I am

rather tired and will have to go to bed now.

Monday

Sir James Goldsmith, who is incredibly rich and a friend of
Mrs Thatcher, says we must have a referendum on the Euro.
Otherwise he will put up candidates in every constituency. I
want everyone to know that I am not afraid of him. Oh no. I
will not be told what to do by any rich businessman. "What
about Mr Heseltine?" asked my wife Norman. "He will not be
told what to do either," I said. Today I spelled out my total
opposition to a referendum in the following no-nonsense
words: "I am not ruling out a referendum. But I would not
rule it in either. I have made our position absolutely clear.
The decision as to whether we rule in or rule out or neither
will be taken at a time that has yet to be ruled in or ruled
out." When I told this to Mr Clarke he was not inconsiderably
annoyed. He told me: "If you decide to have a referendum, I
will resign at once." I managed to calm him down by saying
that there was no question of having a referendum, unless we
decide to have one. This seemed to satisfy him.

Tuesday

I see in the newspapers that I am going to have a reshuffle
in July, and that Sir Patrick Mayhew is going to be rewarded
for all his work on the peace process by being sacked. Sir
Patrick rang me at once to ask whether this was true. I told
him I had no idea and that he should talk to Mr Dr
Mawhinney because he is in charge of all the press releases.
Sir Patrick demanded to know whether I was going to have a

reshuffle or not. "I have made my position on this absolutely clear," I told him. "I have not ruled it out and I have not ruled it in. I shall decide on the ruling in or ruling out when…" Mr Mayhew must have dropped the phone at this point because it went dead.

Wednesday

I am in a place called Egypt. It is very hot and there is a great deal of sand but otherwise I am not sure why we have come. Mr Clinton is here as well, also Mr Bruton from Ireland. I asked him what we were doing here: "We are having our photograph taken," he explained. Mr Clinton then made a speech to all the American journalists saying "Mah fellow Americans, vote for me. As you can see, I am a world statesman." We all clapped and then one of Mr Clinton's aides handed him a piece of paper. "Oh, yes," he said, "we are all united in the fight against terrorism." I asked him why, in that case, he had given a visa to Mr Gerry Adams, but unfortunately Mr Clinton did not hear. In the photograph I was put next to Sheikh N'Vaq who is the Deputy Foreign Minister of the United Arab Sultanate of the South Gulf States. He told me he was a great friend of Mr Aitken and had stayed at his health farm in a place called Berkshire. "Very good jig-jig-jig," he said with a wink, which I took to be a reference to the bicycle machines they have in those places.

Thursday

Back home to find the European Court has made a not inconsiderably silly ruling that British people must work 48 hours a week. As I pointed out to the Cabinet, the latest figures show that over two million Britons now work *no* hours a week at all! How then, I asked, can they obey this ludicrous order from Brussels? The Cabinet all looked very embarrassed, especially Mr Clarke who said: "Sometimes I give up, John."

This is true. He does give up, but then I persuade him to stay on again. That is the real skill of being Prime Minister.

Friday

Even my patience is at last beginning to wear out with the newspapers. They have printed another of those ridiculous polls showing that Mr Blair is 68 points ahead, and that only 1 per cent of the electorate think that I am not "fairly/utterly useless". There is obviously not a shred of evidence for these absurd figures, since we won hands down over the Scott

Report and everyone still remembers how silly Mr Blair was made to look when Mrs Harman did whatever it was she did.

Saturday

We are definitely going to win the next election thanks to my brilliant new initiative to help small businesses. Today Mr Mawhinney has written an article by me in the *Daily Mail* saying that I understand the problems of small businessmen, because my father went bankrupt in 1958 through making garden ornaments and I want everyone else to have the same chance. My brother Terry rang up on his mobile from the gates to Downing Street. "What are these ornaments you keep on going on about, John?" he said. "Why can't you call a gnome a gnome? And, anyway, we know why Dad went bankrupt, don't we? Because of that batch you made that went to Bleasdale's with the wrong coloured hats." As usual, Terry had got it completely wrong. "It was not Bleasdale's but Prendergast's," I told him, "and there was nothing wrong with the hats at all. If anything was wrong it was the fishing rods, which were your department, and which due to defective packing broke off in transit." I have now drawn a line under the garden ornament issue once and for all, oh yes.

April

Monday

Spring is here and the signs of our recovery are everywhere. Oh yes. We have weathered the Scott report and all the other reports. Labour's standing in the opinion polls is falling so fast that it has already been cut to a humiliating 68 points ahead. From now on it is plain sailing down the fast lane to the next election, and if Mr Blair thinks he is going to be prime minister he will have to wait until the cows come home.

Tuesday

My friend Mr Dorrell made a routine announcement in the House of Commons today about a disease called BSE and CJD. I did not understand all the technical details, but the gist of it is that, although it is possible that millions of people are going to die of eating beef, they haven't got any evidence for it. I found this very reassuring and congratulated him on handling a difficult situation very well.

Wednesday

Once again the media have got it all wrong. All the papers this morning had huge headlines about Mr Dorrell's purely routine announcement about millions of people dying because of beef, and demanding that my government should do something. I immediately took very firm and decisive action, as befits a true leader. I asked Mr Heseltine to call a Cabinet meeting so that they can tell me what to do. Mr Hogg said that if nothing was done hundreds of businesses would go bust and thousands of jobs would be lost. "So what?" I said. "There's nothing new about that. It has been part of my policy all along. It is what they call the Feelgood Factor." But Mr Hogg then said that the best thing to do was to kill every single cow in Britain, so that it would be safe to eat beef again, because there wouldn't be

COOPED UP DAIRY

any. The only problem with this would be that it could cost £100 billion which as Mr Clarke pointed out would mean that we could not afford any tax cuts in order to win the next election. At this point everyone realised that this was a really serious crisis and that something would have to be done. But after several hours discussion no one could think of anything.

Thursday

The country has gone mad, but not from eating beef. This morning every page of every newspaper was about how we are all going to die because of this disease. The television is even worse and Mr Humphrys has been screaming for hours that something must be done. I even got a phone call from my brother Terry to ask whether it was safe for his wife Shirley to make him mince for tea, as that was what they always have on Thursday. "When are you going to give us a statement, John?" he asked. I realised that we must act soon, so I told Mr Dorrell to make another statement to calm everyone down, as his first statement had been so effective. He did so at once and told the Commons that there was absolutely nothing to worry about as the risk of millions of people dying was pretty small, although the scientists had no evidence one way or the other. At once Mrs Harman became completely hysterical, screaming and shouting and blaming me personally for not doing anything. "I *am* doing something," I said, quick as a flash. "I am blaming you and the Labour Party for this whole disaster. Not that it is a disaster, oh no. It is all under control."

Friday

I am not inconsiderably incandescent with no small measure of rage, according to the *Daily Telegraph*. Now the EU has decided to interfere in how they run our country by saying that Britain will not be allowed to sell any beef to anywhere in the world ever again. Mr Rifkind came in with a white

face and said: "It's a blanket ban, prime minister." "This is intolerable!" I said. "First beef and now blankets."

Saturday

Fortunately I have a chance to tell all those Europeans exactly what I think of them, as today I had to fly to a place called Tureen, which is where they invented soup. Everyone was there, including Mr Herr Kohl, Mr Monsieur Chirac, Mr Sir Leon Brittan, Mr Herr Kinnock and all the others connected with Europe. I told them that beef would have to be top of the agenda, followed by fish. They agreed to this unconditionally, on condition that we did not discuss either beef or fish issues. After five hours discussing Herr Kohl's very interesting plans for a European superstate, we adjourned for lunch where the menu was as follows:

Greek Olives

Belgian Pâté

Spanish Fish

French Beef

German Sausage

Dutch Cheese

Danish Pastries

"All British dishes have been removed from the menu for health reasons under Directive 96/421," said the waiter with a grin. "I am only obeying orders from Reichsfuherer Herr Kohl," he added in a whisper, raising his arm in a funny way just like Mr Cleese used to do in my wife Norman's favourite programme. Who said foreigners don't have a sense of humour?

Sunday

Mr Mawhinney tells me that Mr Blair is challenging me to a TV duel. "It will be just like Bruno and Tyson," I said. "It will be over in seconds." "Don't be so hard on yourself," said Mr Mawhinney. "You might last a bit longer than Frank."

As usual he had missed the point. I am not worried by Mr Blair, it is just that I am too busy to engage in publicity stunts of this sort.

"What are you doing then?" asked Mr Mawhinney, looking at my Ryman's diary which had a number of blank spaces between Monday and Friday for the next few months.

"Very well," I said. "I will go on television just to show who is boss."

"No, don't do that," he said. "Just go on."

My brother Terry rang me to give me some advice on being on television.

"Don't try and be too clever, John," he said. "Jus be yourself."

Saturday

The mad cow crisis is over. I have finally drawn line under it.

Sunday

We have had a message from our friends in Europe saying they will not allow us to sell any British beef anywhere in the world. But they are prepared to help us out by selling us as much European beef as we need. "This shows how well Europe works," I told my wife Norman, "with everyone pulling in the same direction."

"Against Britain, you mean..." she said, as usual entirely missing the point. "What's for supper?" I asked her, changing the subject. "We are having veal cutlets," she said. "Oh good," I said. "That at least has nothing to do with cows."

Monday

Unfortunately our European friends have still failed to realise that I have solved the beef crisis. I have sent Mr Hogg to Brussels to make our final offer. We will slaughter all the cows in Britain, if they will pay us for it. They came back with a counter-offer that they will pay for it so long as we give them the money first. Also they will never lift the ban. Mr Hogg who is a brilliant negotiator accepted these terms in full. Tonight for supper we had something called Cheval Steak. I was so hungry after waiting all day for Mr Hogg to come back in triumph that I told Norman "I could eat a horse." "That's lucky," she said, "you just have."

Tuesday

I am not inconsiderably incandescent with rage at my friend Mr Clinton. He has apparently given a visa to Mr Blair to go to America, and has even let it be known that he will shake hands with him for the photographers. This is a real betrayal and could well put my election process in jeopardy.

Dr Mawhinney, however, has come to the rescue once again, as he always does. He rushed into by office this morning waving a document and shouting "We've got him this time." It was an amazing secret document from the *Daily Telegraph* cuttings library showing that in 1960 Mr Blair had proposed a motion in his school debating society that "this house believes that nuclear weapons are jolly dangerous." As Dr Mawhinney explained: "This proves that Blair is a 100 per cent anti-American Soviet sympathiser. If we fax this to Clinton, Blair will probably be arrested at the airport." "Good," I told the doctor, "this will really backfire on Blair."

Wednesday

"Pathetic Major Smear on Blair Backfires," said the front page of the *Daily Telegraph*, getting it all wrong as usual. Still, at least they aren't going on about cows. "What is your policy on cows?" asked Norman, as she placed some ostrich rissoles from M and S into the microwave. "Putting your head in the sand in the hope that the whole thing will go away?" At that moment my brother Terry rang reverse-charge from Sydney, which is in Australia. "G'day, you pommie bastard," he said, "I am at the World Garden Ornament Trade Fair Gnome '96". "I am in no small measure not interested in where you are," I said. "I have the biggest crisis since the Falklands on my hands." "Are you sending in a task force to kill all the cows?" he replied. "No," I told him sternly, "they will all be incinerated in the normal manner and then thrown into the sea to be eaten by the fish." "Oh no," said Terry. "So we're all going to end up with Mad Fish Disease?" At this point I decided it was time to draw a line under Terry's phone call and I resumed my conversation with Norman instead. "I think you will find that my policy on cows *is* working," I said. "Unlike everyone in the farming industry," she replied. I decided to finish my rissoles in silence.

Thursday

My friend Mr Clarke tells me that we are going to win the by-election in Staffordshire. He has been down to the constituency and says there is definitely a feelgood factor. "They are feeling good about voting Labour," he explained, "and I felt good as soon as I got on the train home."

Mr Mawhinney said that unfortunately I was too busy to visit Staffordshire myself.

"What am I doing?" I asked him. "You are doing everything you can to help win the by-election," he said, "ie staying in your office.

Friday

We have done not inconsiderably very well in the by-election, easily beating the Liberal Democrats and Screamin' Lord Goldsmith. The excellent result was as follows:

Brigadier C.J.B.Trimbledon-Fyffe (Labour)	39,785
Basil Basildon (Con)	2,112
Oddjob (Screamin' Referendum)	1,136
Shirley Pencil (LibDem)	2

Swing to Labour: 110%

As you can see, the Conservatives are on their way!

The newspapers have of course got the by-election entirely wrong. They are claiming that I lost, which is ridiculous! I still have one more seat than Mr Blair, so I am still the winner.

"If one man dies then the Tories are finished," said the *Daily Telegraph.*

"Not if that man is you," said Mr Mawhinney loyally.

My friend Jeffrey Archer rang me to congratulate me on the by-election and also to tell me that his new novel has won an Oscar, even though he has not written it yet. Hugh Grant has agreed to play the part of the hero, Godfrey Bowman, the millionaire novelist and statesman who has never been to Shepherds Market and certainly did not look at any faxes to his wife Mary before he bought some shares in Anglia TV for a friend.

In the story, apparently, Mr Bowman helps to save the Prime Minister, James Colonel, who is under threat from a sinister billionaire called Sir John Silversmith.

The Prime Minister is so grateful to Bowman that he resigns, appointing Godfrey as his successor.

"This is a terrific story," I told Jeffrey. "It's a pity I don't have any time to read it."

"You will," he said mysteriously.

May

Saturday

I am in my judgement incandescent with rage. The reason that these European foreigners will not buy British beef is that the British government said that it wasn't safe. My wife Norman said we should be pleased, because at least someone believed something that we said. Now Mr Herr Franz Fischler, who is an Austrian gentleman with a beard, says that although our beef is quite safe to eat, he has decided it is unsafe, so the ban stays until we have killed all our cows and then they will buy them again (although not of course the ones that have been killed).

Sunday

Today I had to go to Moscow to have my photograph taken with President Yeltsin and Mr Clinton. Before I left I told Mr Heseltine: "You are in charge." "I know," he said. "Please stop coming in here and telling me what I know already." When I arrived in Moscow I was met by Mr Yeltsin, who was swaying around doing a funny Russian dance. "Ah, Mister Major," he said, "how good of you both to come." Then we did the photograph, with me at the end next to the Deputy Finance Minister of Canada, Jean-Claude Moosejaw. "Thank you, gentlemen," said Mr Yeltsin. "This should help us all get re-elected." "Too late for some of us, eh John?" said Mr Clinton, giving me one of his funny winks. He must have been referring to his imminent defeat at the hands of Senator Blair! On the plane home they were giving away free copies of the *Sunday Express*. I was in no small measure shocked to see on the front page that I had described our partners in Europe as "A Bunch of Shits". As soon as I got back I summoned Dr Mawhinney and went to his office to demand a full explanation. "How did such a terrible word come to be printed?" I asked him. "It must be a misprint. Surely what I said is that they are a

'bunch of suits'?" Dr Mawhinney, who is called "doctor" because he is a spin doctor, laughed and said: "That was no misprint, John. *I* told them you'd said that. It is part of your new 'Get tough with Europe' image." "But I would never use language like that," I told him. "You are a complete shit."

Monday

Mr Mawhinney has put me right in the shit by using that word I would never use. What a shit he is. Everybody is very offended. Even Terry rang up to say: "What a good thing father is not still alive to hear a son of his use the S-word. I had to hide our copy of the *Sunday Express* from Shirley, and we were forced to read a decent family newspaper instead, i.e. the *News of the World.*"

When I turned on the radio at lunchtime to hear whether Mr Botham has become chairman of the England selectors, I was very interested to hear that Mr Heseltine had declared war on Europe for banning our beef. "If they will not buy our beef we will not buy their fruit," he said. "We shall fight them on the peaches, we shall never surrender." This was a very heartwarming message to hear. "At last," I told Norman, "someone has the guts to speak for England."

When we listened to the 2 o'clock news, Mr Rifkind had joined in saying that if the EU wanted to fight dirty, he could play that game as well. He would tell his wife never to buy a single French Golden Delicious apple ever again. By 3 o'clock even Mrs Shephard had added her support to the new get-tough line, saying that she would not be going on any more agreeable holidays in the Dordogne until August.

These threats were so effective in terrifying the Europeans into not lifting their ban, that by the evening Mr Heseltine was able to call off the war. On the Channel Four News he was very statesmanlike, saying to Mr Snow: "Once again you people are making a big fuss

KEEP ON THE GRASS

about nothing. Where did you get this nonsense from about banning fruit? We believe in diplomacy, co-operation and reasoned discussion, so shut your face, you leftie scum." Mr Snow had no answer to this and sat there in silence for at least half a minute with his mouth open.

Tuesday

Today all the papers are full of interviews with the well-known businessman Mr Sir James Goldsmith, who says that he is going to stand at the next election in every constituency at once, on the question of Europe. He says that I am a pathetic wimp who does not stand for anything. Well I have news for him. I will not *stand* for this, oh no! (This joke was written for me by my script writer Mr Morris Norris.) Even the *Daily Telegraph* has written a carefully coded editorial, headed "This Pathic Wimp" saying that I should resign at once. I have decided to make a brilliant speech which will go down in history by making my position on Europe absolutely clear once and for all.

Wednesday

Today I made my historic speech to thousands of businessmen in the Albert Hall, called after Mr Albert Hall who was presumably a well-known businessman. These are the points I made:

1. We are totally committed to Europe.

2. But Europe has been a disaster for Britain in many ways.

3. However it is absolutely right that we are in it, and we have every intention of coming out.

4. The right place for Britain to be is in the fast lane, but strictly observing the speed limit however many flashing lights there are telling you to get out of the way.

5. I have now drawn a very firm line under where I stand on Europe, so we will not hear any more from Mr Goldsmith and his friends.

Thursday

My friend Lord Jeffrey Archer rang me up to tell me about a survey he has done.

"You are going to lose the election," he said. "Thanks to Mr Goldsmith. You cannot afford to ignore very rich tycoons who are interested in politics. They have a lot to offer, and I think you should do a deal with me — I mean him — at once."

Friday

Apparently the health minister Mr Dorrell is going to be the next Prime Minister.

"What rubbish!" I said to my wife Norman when she read it out over our breakfast of Marmite Tea with toast and Goldsmith's "Sir" Jam. "Dorrell is a nonentity who has just made a spectacular mess of everything he is supposed to be in charge of."

"Then he has all the right qualifications," she replied, opening a jar of Gentleman Jimmy's Fishpaste.

"You should try some of this, John," she said. "Everyone's turning to it."

Saturday

I am looking forward to the local elections. Oh yes. At last the country has a chance to show Mr Blair what it thinks of him!

Sunday

Tomorrow will be another of the many historic days in my premiership. Mr Herr Kohl, the German Chancellor, is coming to Britain to discuss peace terms in the great beef war. As Mr Morris Norris explained to me: "It is just like Munich, only the other way round." He even suggested a very good joke for me to tell the journalists when we came out to have our photographs taken. "Why don't you say, prime minister," he suggested, " 'It is beef in our time'?"

Monday

Mr Herr Kohl arrived and to show him what we think of Europe I specially asked the cook (not the one I didn't have an affair with, oh no) to serve the following menu:

British Beef Soup

Side of Best British Beef

Jelly, made from British gelatin

Cream from British BSE-accredited herds

Beef Tea

or

Fish

Unfortunately, Herr Kohl chose the fish, which rather spoiled Mr Norris's joke about the beef, as "Fish in our time" is not nearly as amusing, especially since we had to buy it from the Spanish fish shop El Pesces di Knightsbridge.

Tuesday

Today I made a historic speech about all the loonies, bastards, rebels and other barmies two apples short of a picnic, i.e. Mr Sir James Goldsmith, who do not understand my clear vision of Europe. Mr Norris came up with a brilliant new phrase which really describes Mr Goldsmith and his new

friend Mr Redwood perfectly, i.e. they are all cuckoo. There is indeed no other word to describe these cuckoos. They are completely cuckoo, living on Cloud Nine, which is the place where cuckoos live, when they are not in their nests of course. When I told my wife Norman about my brilliant "cuckoo" idea, she asked: "Is that the cuckoo you didn't have the affair with?" — missing the point as usual.

Wednesday

As usual, the newspapers have got everything wrong. They say I have done a secret deal with Mr Heseltine, so that if I do badly in the local elections he will take over the government. While I was reading this, Mr Heseltine called me into his office and I did not even have to wait for the green light. "What's this about me taking over after the local elections?" he said. "Don't they realise I took over months ago. Now get out and get on with your work!" He is certainly a very decisive man, just what this country needs.

Thursday

Today I have won a great victory in the local elections. All the anti-Conservative press, like the *Daily Mail* and the *Telegraph*, said that we would not win a single seat. How totally wrong can you get. We did win a single seat, in Basildon, which has long been known as one of the safest Labour strongholds in the country. Of course, it was predictable that the Liberals would do well in their traditional heartlands like Tunbridge Wells, but in general it was a night of Tory triumph. When I congratulated

Dr Mawhinney he was so moved that tears began to roll down his cheeks and he jumped out of the window in joy, like my ex-friend Mr Lamont used to do in the days when Britain was doing so well in the ERM.

Friday

Labour are in no small measure on the run after their trouncing at the polls. Dr Mawhinney has discovered three schools in Labour-held parts of London where none of the children can read. "This is a devastating indictment," he said, "of the total failure of Labour's education policy during the last 17 years." No wonder Mr Blair is sending his children to Eton.

Saturday

Today is Europe Day, which is traditionally when we are meant to celebrate the EU. I have decided to use this to send a very clear signal to Brussels of where we now stand on Europe. Instructions have been issued to all departments as follows:

1. EU flags are to be purchased by all departments. This is to show Britain's determination to be at the heart of Europe.

2. These flags are on no account to be flown or waved in any circumstances. This is to show where Britain stands on the beef issue.

Sunday

At last Labour are finished! The newspapers are full of the row between Mr Brown and Mr Mandelson.

I called Dr Mawhinney to tell him the good news.

"The Party is fragmented! They're at each other's throats! They can't agree on a single policy."

"Typical," said Dr Mawhinney. "They're stealing all our ideas again. No wonder they are so far ahead in the polls."

Meanwhile my friend Mr Clark has given an interview to the Observer newspaper. He has had a brilliant idea i.e. **not** to cut taxes. "This will win the next election," I told

Dr Mawhinney. "Yes it will," he replied. "For Labour." He is getting very confused nowadays, due to working too hard.

When I spoke to Mr Clark he made it very clear. "Of course, Prime Minister," he said, "this will be an unpopular measure in the short term. But in the long term it will be of huge benefit to the Party when they are returned to power with a new Prime Minister, one who is a man of principle, one who refuses to cut taxes just to be popular, one who wears suede shoes, likes jazz and smokes Panatellas."

Poor Mr Clark! He does not realise that I have black shoes, like Buddy Holly and do not smoke at all. He must be working too hard as well.

Monday

Today it was Mr Monsieur Chirac's turn to come to Britain to eat beef. First we arranged for him to do a number of other things, like review the British Army, ride around in a carriage and meet the Queen, but then came the really important bit when we invited him to lunch at Downing Street and showed him the menu. This time we had learned our lesson, oh yes. When Mr Herr Kohl came, he was offered English beef or Spanish fish, and he chose the fish. But this time the menu was as follows:

Boeuf Anglais

or

Beef Wellington

or

English Beef.

To follow:

Ice Cream and Gelatine Anglaise.

Mr Herr Chirac thanked me very much in perfect English, and said: "That is very kind of you, mon brave, but I have brought some fishpaste sandwiches." Obviously Mr Herr Kohl had warned him!

Tuesday

Mr Doctor Mawhinney has come up with a brilliant new slogan which will win us the next election and make everyone forget about beef. He has put up huge posters all over London reading: "We Aren't Any Good But Vote For Us Anyway." He says it combines humour with humility, which is exactly what the voters want according to a survey done by one of our marketing firms, Fowler and Mellor Associates. Apparently, when people were asked what they thought of the government, 98 per cent said: "They are a complete joke, who ought to be begging our forgiveness for cocking everything up." It is good to see Mr Mawhinney on top of his job!

Wednesday

Today I had to go out to Ryman's to buy a special new book for the "Beef Bastards". This is all the Europeans who last night voted against me on the lifting of the ban on sallow, teamen and gelignite which are all made from British beef. The first name in the book is Mr Herr Kohl who is the biggest bastard of all. He promised to vote for us and when it came to it, he didn't. What a bastard. I am now not inconsiderably totally furious with these foreigners. After all I have done defending them against Mrs Gorman and Mr Portaloo. I have decided after very careful thought that I am so angry that there is only one thing left to do. I am going to declare war on Europe, just like Mr Chamberlain did in 1939. I will not even have to ask Mr Heseltine's permission, since he is on a very important visit to China and has left me holding the fort while he is away.

Thursday

Today the House of Commons witnessed the most historic speech since Mr Churchill told the Europeans that we would fight them on the peaches. At precisely 3.17 pm I stood up and said that Britain had had enough. "That is why," I said, "I have decided that, as of now, this country is officially in a state of non-cooperation with our European partners." There was a hushed silence at these historic words, broken only by a lone cheer from Mrs Teresa Gorman (note: I must take her name out of the Bastards Book — not my new Beef Bastards book, but the other one). Then Mr Blair stood up and as usual tried to catch me out by asking: "What exactly are you going to do?" "What a typically pathetic question," I responded, quick as a flash. "You are really pathetic to ask me that." This shut him up, and he immediately jumped up again with his in no small measure irritating smile and asked "So what are you going to do then?" "We are going to do nothing at all," I told him, "that is what non-co-operation means."

Friday

Today we had one of our best Cabinet meetings since the Falklands crisis. This morning for the first time for years all the newspapers (even Labour papers like the *Sun* and the *Express*) were solidly behind us. I decided to celebrate by going into our Cabinet meeting wearing a Union Jack waistcoat, which Mr Mawhinney had brought for me from a stall on Oxford Street. Much to my surprise, when I got into the Cabinet room, I found Mr Portaloo and Mr Rifkind were wearing them too — in fact everyone except Mr Waldegrave who was wearing his special Pop waistcoat from Eton and Mrs Bottomley who was wearing a National Lottery teeshirt bearing the slogan "Give Us Your Money and We'll Give It To Camelot." After we had sung Land of Hope and Glory, I told everyone that I was going to move into Mr Churchill's war bunker and would be directing the great Beef War (codenamed Operation Oxocube) myself. I would be appointing a special War Cabinet within the Cabinet, which would consist of everyone in the Cabinet except Mr Hogg, who cannot be trusted because he got us into this mess in the beginning. In his place I have appointed my new friend Mr Freeman as Supreme Commander of Allied Forces (Beef). Trying to be difficult, as usual, Mr Clark asked me who our allies were. I immediately snapped back: "What a pathetic question. You are

really pathetic, worse than Mr Blair." This really showed them all that I am a strong leader who will not be messed around by anybody, whether European, or in the Cabinet. To make my point, I ordered Mr Waldegrave to go out at once to get himself a patriotic waistcoat like everyone else, except Mrs Bottomley.

June

THE SECRET WAR DIARY OF JOHN MAJOR
Supreme Commander of B.E.F.
(Beef Export Forces)

TOP SECRET
Not to be read until 2096

Monday

The war is going very well on all fronts. Today in my War Room deep below Whitehall we put a map of Europe on the table, and stuck little cows on the end of rulers, just like Mr Churchill used to do in the last war (except with boats and tanks obviously instead of cows). At the moment all our cows are massed along the South Coast in secret positions, waiting for my signal for when the ban is lifted and they can sweep across the Channel. Mr Dr Mawhinney had the brilliant idea of calling it "C Day" instead of D-Day. In the meantime, Mr Freeman was able to report a whole string of glorious victories in our battle against our European allies.

1. Britain abstains in key vote setting Greek octopus quota.

2. Britain blocks the Harmonisation of Laws on Photocopying Directive, a pet project of the Portuguese trade minister Senhor Xavier Xerox.

3. British delegate deliberately falls asleep during debate on subsidies to Finnish Windfarms, thus bringing proceedings to an early halt at 3.26 am.

And this is only the beginning of my campaign which, if necessary, we will keep going for hundreds of years.

Tuesday

I have decided to take a secret holiday behind enemy lines in a place called Cannes which is in France. I am travelling incognito as plain "John Major" and so far not a single person has recognised me. Today my wife Norman and I made a recce of the local butcher's shops, which are called "boulangeries", to see whether the French were eating beef. With the aid of my old school French dictionary I asked the manager: "Excusez-moi, mon bonhomme, êtes-vous vendant du boeuf?" At this he told me politely that he didn't sell any meat of any kind. I had not realised how bad things have got.

Wednesday

Today I had a very busy day. First I had to sack someone called Mr Richards whom I had never heard of. Apparently one of the papers has said that he was having an affair with a dog lady, which of course is totally contrary to our principles of family values. As I told the Cabinet: "It is all right not to have an affair with someone, like I didn't with the cook. But it is not all right to have an affair with someone like this dog lady." The Cabinet looked very thoughtful at my very sensible words, and eventually Mr Heseltine asked: "What if someone like this friend of mine who is in the Cabinet is having an affair, but he manages to keep it out of the papers?" "Oh, that's all right," I said. "That's completely different."

Then Mr Arafat, who is the leader of the Palestinians, came to have his photograph taken and then stayed to lunch.

We had planned to give him beef, but since so many world statesmen seem not to like beef, we gave him pork instead. Mr Arafat was very unhappy about his peace process. "It is all in ruins," he said, wiping his eyes with the towel on his head, "because the extremists won the election." "At least that cannot happen to my peace process here in Britain," I told him, without trying to sound too smug.

Thursday

Oh dear. We have just heard the results of the elections in Northern Ireland. They are as follows:

G. Adams (Guns For Peace/Sinn Fein)	16 per cent
Rev. Mr Dr I. Paisley (Sod the Pope Unionist)	57 per cent
D. Kneetremble (Official Responsible Moderate Sensible Unionist)	1 per cent
J. Hume (Official Moderate Responsible Sensible Nationalist)	1 per cent
Conor Cruise O'Booze (Red Faced Imitators of Paul Johnson For Peace)	1 per cent
Mairead O'Feminism (Women Against Male Violence Alliance)	1 per cent
Other Parties (370 in all)	4 per cent

Under my very clever scheme, everyone will have a seat at the peace talks except Mr Adams. This way my peace process will continue. Of that, let there be no doubt. Oh no.

Friday

To keep the enemy guessing in the beef war, the War Cabinet has decided on a secret weapon. We are going to launch Mr Hogg round the capital cities of Europe on a "charm offensive". To show this on the map, we have sellotaped a plastic Batman from my Sugar-Frosted Shreddies on the end of a pencil, as we have run out of rulers. We told Mr Hogg to throw away his silly hat and scruffy mac, and to buy a new suit from Marks and Spencer's, and whatever he does, he must smile at all times. "Why must I do that?" he said. "Because otherwise I will sack you," I said in my very stern, Churchill-in-1940 voice. "But I have not had an affair with anyone," he complained.

Saturday

We were very pleased to see Mr Hogg on the news today walking up to Mr Santer in Brussels and slapping him on the back with the words "Guten abend Herr Kohl — how about lifting the ban so I can keep my job, ha, ha, ha."

Sunday

Unfortunately, Mr Santer does not seem to have understood Mr Hogg's charm offensive, or rather he has only understood the "offensive" part of it, since he has now issued a statement saying that he was sick of the "silly little English being xenophobes". He explained that if the British policy was not to co-operate with Europe until the beef ban was lifted, his answer was simple. "We will not lift the beef ban until Britain co-operates." This is very good news because it shows that we have really got Europe worried. As I told the Cabinet, "Our slogan should be, 'Oh yes, it's hurting, even though it's not working'."

Monday

Today is a historic day for Northern Ireland as my peace talks begin. Mr Bruton and I went on television to distract attention from Mr Adams who was complaining about not being allowed in.

Unfortunately when we went into the talks he was still outside being filmed by the television people, which was in no small measure annoying.

There are 60 delegates from nine parties and two governments. There is also a Finnish politician, a Canadian general and an American senator.

With all this expertise round the table, I am sure we will be able to solve the immediate problems — i.e. where we are all going to sit.

Unfortunately Mr Paisley decided that he would not come to the talks because he does not like the American gentleman.

"Shall we start the talks?" I began in my statesmanlike voice. "Now that we are all here except the Unionists and the Republicans..."

Everybody started laughing, which showed that there was a good positive atmosphere there.

Tuesday

My beef war continues with victories on all fronts! Today in my War Room I was able to write up on my special War Blackboard a list of the latest measures we have been able to block:

1. Proposal to extend VAT to dried snails.

2. Council Regulation to harmonise teabag perforations throughout the EU.

3. Resolution to outlaw nodding dogs over 32.5mm in vehicle rear windows as a safety hazard.

It can now only be a matter of time before our European partners are offering us terms to surrender.

Wednesday

Another victory, this time on the home front. The Euro-sceptics are completed routed. I found out that one of their leaders, Mr Cash, was secretly getting money from Mr Sir James Goldsmith a very rich Europhobe who is the leader of a new party that is going to lose me the next election. Not that we are going to lose, oh no. Anyway, I called Mr Cash into my study, just like my old headmaster Mr Brownlow used to do (he was not called Mr Wilkins as certain totally inaccurate writers,i.e.Terry, have claimed in their books, which I haven't read). "Mr Cash," I said. "You are a bastard. Unless you stop taking money from the traitor Goldfish, I will put you in my Bastard book, along with Mrs Gorman and Mr Redwood." Poor Mr Cash. He is such a weed that he cried and cried and eventually promised not to take any more money. "No more Cash!" I shouted as he ran out of the door in tears (this joke was entirely my own and was written for me by Mr Morris Norris). Thanks to my firm and decisive action, I think we have now heard the last of the Euro-Sceptics.

Thursday

I am not inconsiderably incandescent with rage and I might well spontaneously combust with hatred. I have just heard that Mrs Thatcher has invited Mr Cash to lunch to offer him all the money which Mr Sir James Goldfish would have given him. This is the final act of treachery. That woman has no shame. I decided to deal with Mrs Thatcher once and for all by issuing a savage, no-holds-barred attack on her in a press statement. This is what it said: "Lady Thatcher is of course at liberty to donate to whomsoever she wishes. But I do think that it might have been more prudent and appropriate in the current circumstances for her to have used the funds to support the Conservative Party of which she is a member." Oh yes. I read this out to my wife Norman over our patriotic breakfast of Kellogg's Beef Krispies and a cup of Gelatino.

"That'll show Mrs Thatcher who's boss," I told her. "Yes," said Norman. "It certainly will."

Friday

I have received a letter on House of Commons paper written in green ink. "Major," it says, "keep our hospital open or we will close you down. Signed, Two Backbenchers. PS. We know where you live. But you won't for long."

I was speechless to think that members of my party could behave in this way. I told the House of Commons: "Threatening to withdraw co-operation unless your demands are met is nothing short of blackmail."

Later, I wrote to Mr Kohl about the beef issue. I had the very clever idea of cutting some words out of the newspaper and pasting them on a sheet of paper so he would not know who it came from:

"Kohl," it said. "Lift the beef ban or I will close down Europe. Signed, Your Enemy. PS. I know where you live, at 3901 Konigstrasse, Bonn. JM."

Saturday

My letter worked. They have given in. Today I went to Florence, which is in Italy, for a summit and received from the Europeans the terms of their unconditional surrender:

1. The British hereby agree to abandon their policy of non-cooperation immediately.

2. The British agree to slaughter all known cows.

3. After this has been done, the European

Union may agree to consider the possibility of a framework
for lifting the ban by the year 2050.
Signed J. Santer,
pp. EU (prop. H. Kohl)

This is total victory. I have won the war. As I said to
Norman when we were watching the television over a
celebratory patriotic dinner of beef pizza (with Extra Beef
Topping) followed by a tin of Ambrosia's Semenolina pudding:
"Now who's going to win the next election?" At that moment
the screen filled with a shot of Mr Herr Kohl with his arm
round Mr Blair. "There is your answer," she said, once again
showing how little she understands about politics.

Sunday (early)

Needless to say the newspapers have got it entirely wrong,
saying that my triumph in Florence was "a climbdown".
What, in my judgement, rubbish! I said that non-cooperation
would work. And it has. In fact it has worked so well that the
EU have decided to
borrow the idea and
are refusing to co-
operate in lifting
the beef ban!

I phoned Mr
Mawhinney to tell
him that I had now
worked out "a
framework deal"
which meant that
the public would
only have to wait "a
couple of months"
for the good news.

"You're
resigning, are you?"
he asked. Poor Mr
Mawhinney. He must have been eating too much beef!

Mr Kohl later announced on television that he will not end
the beef ban until Mr Blair is prime minister.

"Shall I order a joint for next Sunday then?" asked
Norman, which was unusually thoughtful of her. She has
obviously realised that the feelgood factor is back. Not that it
ever went away. Not only have we won the beef war, but now
we have also won the football by beating Holland 4-1. I sent a

telegram to our team saying: "If you lot can win, then anyone can. Vote Conservative."

Sunday (very late)

As if I did not have enough on my plate (except beef of course), my sister Pat has decided to cash in on my celebrity. My brother Terry rang me at an unearthly hour (i.e. 9.37 pm) saying: "Have you seen the *Telegraph*, John? It looks like Pat is going to be almost as famous as me! The stuff about Mrs Kierans is dynamite!"

This is typical of Terry, who has failed to see that the important issue is not Mrs Kierans but the ownership of Kevin, the angora rabbit.

Let it be clear for the record that there was never any dispute at all over Kevin, as Pat — or Mrs Dessoy, as she now is — alleged. Her article was nearly as inaccurate as Terry's book which of course I have not read.

It was *my* rabbit because I bought the rabbit food from Mrs Wooton's Pet Shop (the pet shop owned by Mrs Wooton in Sandyvale Road).

I hope I have now drawn a line under the whole rabbit incident and we will be hearing no more of Kevin or Mrs Kierans or indeed Mrs Dessoy.

July

Monday

Mr Dr Mawhinney is a genius. Every day he comes up with a new brilliant idea for winning the next election. Last week he put up millions of posters all over the country saying: "Yes, It Hurts. No, It Doesn't Work. Vote Conservative." Today he came in with a new set of slogans which are even more brilliant, and asked me to choose which one was best. They were:

"Now You See It. Now You Don't (Mr Blair)."

"Yes, It's Hurd. No, It's Rifkind."

"Yes, It Works On An Egg. No, It Doesn't."

"This Campaign Isn't Working. Oh, Yes, It Isn't."

Mr Dr Mawhinney said that our new advertising team, run by Mr Saatchi, had been writing round-the-clock for three months to produce all these vote-winning ideas, and they were well worth the £10 million we are paying them.

Tuesday

Today Mr Dr Mawhinney had another brilliant idea for winning the next election when he rang up to say that I was going to the final of the football competition. "It will be a great photo-opportunity, John," he said, "and a chance for 5 billion people to see that, although we were beaten by the Germans in the semi-final, we don't hold a grudge against them." "Yes," I said, "it will show that we are very good losers." "Don't say that," said Mr Dr Mawhinney in his jokey voice, "you'll ruin everything you idiot". I have to say that I enjoyed watching the Germans win. "But then you're used to that," said my wife Norman, as she served up our late night, post-match herbal tea (cinnamon and vegetable marrow).

Wednesday

I was in no small measure not very pleased when I saw in the *Daily Telegraph* that my sister Mrs Dessoy (whom I have not seen for 20 years) has written another article under the headline "My Bonking Brother's Naughty Nights With Dirty Divorcee — A Telegraph Exclusive." I immediately called in Mr Dr Mawhinney and told him that this kind of thing was very damaging. "Yes," he said, "to Mr Blair. It was all my idea. There you are, all over the front pages. Jack the Lad, Men Behaving Badly — it makes you into Nineties Man, unlike Holy Joe Blair with his Christian Socialism and his holier-than-thou Communion chasing. This one's really going to do the trick, John," he said.

Thursday

The latest poll shows unfortunately that since the revelations by my sister about Mrs Kierans, my rating has slipped another 10 points, from 5 to minus 5. When I showed this to Mr Dr Mawhinney, he said: "Don't worry, John, just look at today's idea." He showed me a very fat book called *The Road To Ruin* which he explained was a very funny parody of the Labour Party manifesto for the next election. He and Mr Heseltine are going to read out the jokes, which go like this:

HESELTINE: I say, I say, I say. Knock, knock.

MAWHINNEY: Who's there?

HESELTINE: New Labour.

MAWHINNEY: Don't let them in — they're very dangerous.

HESELTINE: Ha, ha, ha. I say, Brian, how many New Labour men does it take to change a lightbulb?

MAWHINNEY: None, because they prefer to keep everyone in the dark. (I thought this one was my favourite. It was apparently written by none other than Sir David Frost. As I told Norman later, he is definitely one of the funniest men in England. "But not the funniest," she said, giving me one of her looks.)

There were plenty more hilarious jokes like these ones, and I very much look forward to reading what the newspapers have to say about the launch tomorrow.

Friday

All the papers have given front-page coverage to our brilliant new campaign. "Embarrassing, Pathetic, Pitiful," "Hezza and Mazza 'Two Ronnies Show' Gets the Bird," "The Joke's on You John — You're The Laughing Stock." It is very clever of Mr Dr Mawhinney to get so much publicity.

Saturday

Mr Dr Mawhinney has really surpassed himself this time. He woke me up at 6 o'clock this morning to say: "Have you seen the Russian news, John?"

I replied that I was far too busy being asleep to watch the television, but he continued: "I've cracked it, John. I've got the secret for winning the election. First you drink a lot of vodka then you go on television looking drunk and dancing about with some pretty girls. Then you get very ill and have to go to bed. Everyone thinks you're dead and so they vote for you." I told Mr Dr Mawhinney that he should go to bed and perhaps call a real doctor.

Sunday

Mr Dr Mawhinney has had his best brilliant idea yet.

He came in today with two tickets for Wembley. "The football is all over," I said to him quick as a flash to show that I know what is going on. "It is the Three Tenors," he told me.

"That is very cheap for Wembley," I said.

"No, you idiot," he joked. "Your wife Norman is very keen on opera. Apparently, she enjoys the spectacle of tragic men coming to bitter ends. This will make you look very cultured and not just someone who likes football."

In the event, it was a very cold and wet evening which consisted entirely of three rich fat Europeans shouting at me in various languages I did not understand. "I might as well go to Brussels," I told Norman.

She did not however seem to hear me as one of the men was singing an Italian song called "Summenchanta Evenin".

When it was all over I said to Norman: "I am very cold and wet". "Correct," she said — rather unnecessarily in my judgement.

Monday

Today I launched my campaign to win the next election by granting an exclusive interview to a lady from the *Daily Telegraph* who has very long legs and an even longer name, i.e. Salmonella Wyfront. Unfortunately, most of the time had to be taken up with arranging the photograph which was to show her sitting on the sofa talking to me. Some of her questions were not inconsiderably personal in tone, eg had I read Terry's book? I had to explain once again that, owing to the pressures of running the country, I had not had time to read it, but that it did contain a very large number of errors, eg on p.183 where it says that I came third from bottom in a maths exam at Rusbridger Grammar School, the maths teacher was wrongly named as Mr Wingate, when as everybody who went to the school knows it was the famous Mr Beamish (whom we all called "The Beamer"). Unfortunately, the *Daily Telegraph* reporter did not have the space in her full page article to correct these errors.

Tuesday

Mr Dr Mawhinney has come up with yet another brilliant slogan to win us the next election — "Have We Got New Labour For You — Yes It Doesn't Work." He tells me it will be used on TV showing an old lady looking out of her window and seeing a huge monster looking like Mr Blair knocking down all the houses opposite. Then a voice says, "It Could Be New — Labour. Vote Conservative." There is no doubt that Dr Mawhinney was an inspired choice to succeed that other man whom I met in the tea room and who used to do the crossword, but whose name I cannot now remember, although his mother

was in my favourite film, *Genevieve* (not *I'm Alright Jack*, as Terry claims on p.261).

Wednesday

I am incandescent with rage. For once the *Daily Telegraph* has got it right. My ex-friend Mr Bruton, the so-called Teasock of Ireland, has accused me of destroying the peace process by allowing some of Mr Paisley's friends to walk down the road in bowler hats blowing whistles and beating drums. Let it be abundantly clear, the decision to allow the march was wholly the fault of the policeman in charge, Mr Annesley. We merely told him to let the march take place, otherwise we would have violence on the streets. But from then on it was entirely an operational decision for Mr Annesley, and the violence on the streets which followed must be laid at his door alone. Oh yes. How dare Mr Bruton say I am to blame for destroying my own peace process, which has been the greatest single achievement of my prime ministership, apart from the Cones Hotline, vouchers for nursery schools and my Maastricht opt-outs. However, I have decided to draw a line under Mr Bruton 's stupid remarks, and in due course I will invite him to take part in new talks about talks about talks.

Thursday

Today we have taken a holiday from politics to celebrate the 80th birthday of one of our most revered and respected statesmen, Mr Sir Edward Heath. Some time ago my wife Norman and I decided to invite him to a special dinner at Number 10, and he replied by sending a list of all the guests he wanted to be present. They included quite a lot of foreigners whom he used to know when he was prime minister, like Mr Pompidou from France, and also what he called "some fellow great musicians", such as Mr Sir Lord Yehudi Menuhin and Mr Rostropologist from Russia.

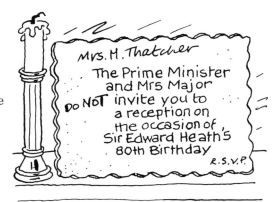

Mrs. M. Thatcher

The Prime Minister and Mrs Major Do NOT invite you to a reception on the occasion of Sir Edward Heath's 80th Birthday

R.S.V.P.

Norman and I were very considerably looking forward to this historic occasion, as I have long felt that Sir Edward and I have a great deal in common — eg, we have both been Conservative prime ministers and we both share a not inconsiderable dislike for that woman whom neither of us ever mention, i.e. Mrs Thatcher.

The party was a great success until Mr Heath began his speech which everyone agreed went on slightly too long, i.e. four hours. It was quite interesting to hear him list all his achievements during his long and distinguished career, such as his repeal of resale price maintenance in 1964, his Local Government Reform Act of 1972 and the introduction of decimal coinage.

Friday

I am not inconsiderably incandescent with pleasure. At last I think things are going our way for the next election. Today the whole of London was in chaos because of a tube strike, and there were no letters because the postmen are also on strike. This is tremendous news, because it really reminds everyone of what life will be like under a Labour Government.

Tonight I was invited to a very historic interview on *News at Ten* with the country's most probing interviewer Mr Trevor Barbados.

As usual, Mr Barbados's questions were very tricky to deal with. For example, when he said to me: "Prime Minister, may I congratulate you on the success of your peace process. You are the bravest man in history," I was momentarily at a loss for words. Oh yes. Then I had an inspiration and, quick as a flash, I replied: "Thank you."

That put him in his place and from then on he was more conciliatory.

Saturday

Today someone else who I had never heard of announced that he was resigning over my policy on the European currency.

How can this man who I have not heard of resign over a policy which does not exist (i.e. I have not made up my mind yet)?

He is obviously a bastard and I will put him in my book as soon as I have discovered what his name is.

August

THE SECRET
OLYMPIC DIARY
OF JOHN MAJOR

Monday

This week begins my secret weapon in the battle to win the next election, ie Britain's performance in the Olympics. I have been to Ryman's in my lunch hour and have bought three special notebooks to record all our medals — a gold one, a silver one and a bronze one. Well, actually they are all grey, but I have written the words "Gold", "Silver" and "Bronze" on them. By the end of this week I confidently predict that the books will be full, the feelgood factor will be back and I will be heading for a "Gold" at the election, with only a silver for Mr Blair and the bronze for Mr Ashdown. Mr Redwood will not even get into the final and Sir James Goldsmith will be disqualified for cheating.

Tuesday

There has been a temporary hiccup in my election-winning plan, codenamed "Going For Gold". Mr Linford Christie has fallen down even before the race started, and I had already written him in my book as the winner of the 100 metres. This is not

inconsiderably annoying. However, I am sure that Miss Sally Gunnell will make up for it tomorrow in the hurdling events.

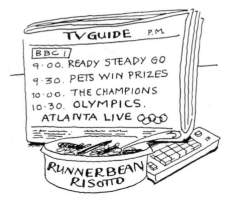

Wednesday

Miss Gunnell has let me down. She has fallen over and sprained her ankle, forcing me to remove her name as well from my "Gold" book. However, it is early days and we still have many winners waiting to claim their medals, eg Colin Jackson in the hurdles and Linford Christie again in the 200 metres, which he will almost certainly win if he doesn't fall down.

Thursday

It has not been a very good day for my great election campaign, or rather night, since all the events seem to take place after my usual bedtime. Mr Christie and Mr Jackson have not done as well as I expected, although Mr Jackson did come fourth, which was very good considering that he was up against some of the best athletes in the world.

Friday

At last a historic day, and I have been able to make full use of my books. Someone called Mr Smith won the bronze in the High Jump, which is the first time an Englishman has won in this event for 60 years. "So you're for the High Jump," said my wife Norman appreciatively, which shows that she is at last beginning to understand politics. Also we got a bronze in the 8000 metres Mountain Bike Pursuit event, which has already put us 69th in the medals table, way ahead of countries such as:

Benin

Pitcairn Island

Rwanda

Vatican City

Antarctica.

Saturday

Gold, gold, gold! Or rather, at least, *one* gold by the two greatest oarsmen in the world, Michael Redgrave and Harold Pinter, or something like that, who are both British. This will show Mr Blair who is boss! I woke Norman to tell her the great news at 2.14am. "What are Coxless Pairs?" she asked. "Two men going down the river very fast, without anyone telling them where to go," I explained. "Just like you and Dr Mawhinney," she said, going back to sleep.

Sunday

There is no stopping us now. We are on course for medals in all the following events:

Underwater Kayak Pairs

Mixed Table Tennis

Men's Hairstyling

Crazy Golf

Beach Scrabble

Marathon Kite-Flying

Synchronised Pot-Holing

Women's 4x4 minute microwaving

The final tally could well be not inconsiderably world-beating, and we might even pull ahead of:

Costa Rica

Bosnia

Outer Mongolia

Muroroa

Sunday

Today the Olympic Games finished with a final result which I have to admit was in my judgement in no small measure not quite as good as I had expected. I have decided to retitle all my books as Gold Bastards, Silver Bastards and Bronze Bastards, with the names of all the people who let me down so badly written in them instead. The situation is so serious that I called in Mr Ian Sport, the Minister of Sproat, and asked him why he hadn't resigned. "Don't you realise," I told him "that I was well on course to win the next election, and now you have thrown it away?" Not that we are going to lose, oh no. But now I will have to think up a new secret weapon.

"Why don't you go on holiday, Prime Minister?" said Mr Sport. "That usually makes you more popular."

This is a good idea, so I have told Norman that we are going off to a country called Algarvia, which did not win any medals at all in the Olympic Games.

Monday

This is not a historic day at all as I am on holiday. My wife Norman and I are in Algarvia staying once again at the Apartmentos Blockos which we share with a number of other charming British couples.

They are all very kindly pretending not to know who I am and are ignoring me.

The only person who has broken this protocol is the German man who runs the local bar, Mr Messerschmidt, who is married to an Englishwoman called Doreen who Norman gets on very well with.

When we went into his bar, which is called "The Trafalgar Arms English Breakfast Served All Day", he said to me: "You are a bloody menace Herr Major. You have ruined my English Sausage Special and Sunday Roast Beef A-GO-A-GO! No one wants to eat Yorkshire Pudding with sardines or prawns! This BSE is all your fault!"

I was in no small measure annoyed with him and told him in no uncertain terms that in future I would find somewhere else to drink in the evenings.

Unfortunately, there isn't anywhere else, so it looks like Norman and I will be staying in and having a lot of early nights (6.30pm).

Tuesday

Mr Dr Mawhinney rang today, which was not inconsiderably annoying, to tell me that the newspapers were full of pictures of Mr Blair walking around Tuscany looking at old churches and art galleries. "Why can't we have some of you doing this?" he asked. "Because I am not in Tuscany," I told him in my especially stern voice. "I am in Algarvia and I am not interested in old churches anyway."

He then told me to get hold of a copy of the *Daily Telegraph* to see his latest poster which had been a great success.

I told him that I was too busy relaxing to worry about this, but later when I went down to the local store, Los Tescos, to buy some insect repellant for myself and some Factor 24 Sun-Block for Norman, I happened to see the headline "Demon Poster A Pathetic Flop For Tories" with a big picture next to it of Mr Blair with red eyes and huge teeth.

Mr Dr Mawhinney's idea has obviously caught on and has made it to the front pages!! Even the local Portuguese newspaper, *The Algarvia Argos*, has featured it as the top story. "Satanicos Blairos — Grandos Blunderos per Majores" it says!

Wednesday

Mr Howard has sent me a fax saying that there were a lot of dangerous people loose in Britain who might vote Labour.

It seems that six of our MPs have refused to ban handguns and that there has been a storm of protest.

Mr Howard says we are presented with a difficult choice.

Do we support our members in their unpopular decision or do we do a quick U-Turn in order to win some votes?

It is certainly a difficult balancing act and so I sent a fax back telling him to jump off at once and consider the second option very carefully.

However, it took me a long time to send the fax because the line was constantly blocked by someone trying to ring me up.

It turned out to be my brother Terry who has got the idea into his head that his book would sell very well in Algarvia and wanted my help to find a distributor.

"You will have to correct all the mistakes," I told him, with no small irritation. "For example, I did *not* buy my Raleigh Kestrel with the 3-speed gears from Peaslands in Sutton High Street as it says on page 151. The bike was a second-hand Humber Sprint from the Wallington Bicycle Shop next to the station. And the pump was extra."

"No one in Portugal will notice the difference," said Terry, to my not inconsiderable annoyance. "It is the broad sweep of the narrative that will carry the reader along — plus, of course, the new chapter about Mrs Kierans."

Thursday

Mr Dr Mawhinney has been on the phone once more causing me yet again to put down my friend Jeffrey Archer's excellent new novel and come inside.

This was in my judgement very annoying since I had just reached the bit where the hero Godfrey Bowman, having written a best-selling book about the tycoon Max Robertwell, becomes Prime Minister by popular demand after a Referendum.

This time Mr Dr Mawhinney had bad news. Mrs Thatcher has decided to speak at the Tory Conference on behalf of the Referendum Party.

"We are doing everything in our power to stop her," he assured me. "So she'll carry on and do it anyway," interrupted Norman, as she changed the blue tablet in the anti-mosquito device. Mr Dr Mawhinney asked me what we should do. I suggested that he produce another one of his posters, this time showing

Mrs Thatcher with mad red eyes, huge teeth and the caption "Old Thatcher. New Danger".

"It is a very good idea, Prime Minister," he said, "and you really must not sit in the sun for too long."

Friday

Mr Howard has now phoned me up to ask my opinion about the identity card.

"I thought I had drawn a line under this one," I told him in my stop-bothering-me-on-holiday voice, which I have not copied from Mr Blair. Oh no.

"These new cards are voluntary, Prime Minister," Mr Howard assured me. "No one will be obliged to have one. It is just that they will be arrested and sent to prison if they don't."

Saturday

On leaving Algarvia airport I was stopped at the desk by a policeman who asked to see my identity card.

"It is purely voluntary," I told him, "and the details have not been worked out yet."

He immediately arrested me and Norman and I missed our plane. In the police station later I asked him: "Do you know who I am?" "No," he said in Portuguese (which is the same word "no") — which proves how essential these cards are even if you are a world-famous statesman.

DEAR BILL

An occasional series of letters from
Denis Thatcher to his old golfing partner
Bill Deedes. Found in No. 10 Downing
Street and marked
'Intercepted and Forwarded by MI5'

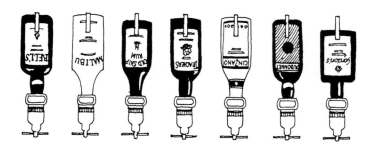

CHESTER SQUARE
LONDON SW1

NOVEMBER 1995

Dear Bill,

I was sorry to miss you at the boss's 70th Birthday do at the
Ritz or was it the Savoy? (They're all the same these days.) I
got cornered by one of the marketing men from Philip Morris
offering me two million bucks to do a commercial for their
fairly revolting gaspers parachuting out of Concorde.

You probably saw that there was a repeat performance by
the Yanks given for some reason in Washington Station and
hosted by Hopalong's emaciated spouse, Nancy. The old boy
failed to show, claiming a general loss of powers due to
Alzheimer's, but, as I said to the E.S., that hadn't stopped me
from donning the bib and tucker.

When we finally sat down I noted that the seat next to the
boss was vacant and that she was having to lean across an
empty chair to catch the E.S.'s pleasantries. I asked that bearded
johnny who used to play God in the Bible films who it was who
had failed to show and he muttered something about a newt
which I took to be a reference to my personal demeanour and
jolly unfair, as it happened, I having by that stage merely
consumed one of those disgusting American shorts called a
Mississippi Buckshot with bits of coconut floating about on
top. The Almighty however explained to me that the absentee
was one Newt (short for Newton) Gingrich, speaker of their

parliament and the boss's number one fan in the US. I said he couldn't be such a big fan if he couldn't be bothered to show up, but just then he trundled in full of apologies — terrible traffic, some ghastly black men's demo bringing the town to a halt, etc, etc. He turned out to be a perfectly reasonable sort of chap, all in favour of abolishing income tax and welfare payments and after the initial froideur he and the boss hit it off like a couple of old buddies, although I don't think she had the faintest idea who he was.

The good news is that the Boy Mark was nowhere to be seen, he and his blonde spouse having packed their bags and hopped it to South Africa where they have purchased a luxury thatched mansion complete with swimming pool and all the trimmings. I rang my friend Mrs Van der Kaffirbasher to ask her to keep an eye on them and warn me of any pending embarrassment to the house of Thatcher, but Mrs Mombolu, her new housekeeper, said she had taken one of her rotties to the vet to have him put down after he bit the neighbour's leg off.

I enclose an encouraging piece from the *Telegraph* saying that alcohol and nicotine help to ward off Alzheimer's. Pity nobody showed it to Hopalong.

Yours, nearly one over the eight,

DENIS

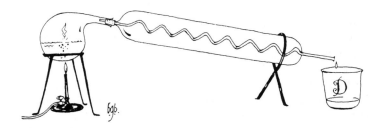

CHESTER SQUARE
LONDON SW1

JANUARY 1996

Dear Bill,

Belated thanks for the book about marital problems for the over-eighties. I tried doing the pelvic exercise on Page 10 and had to go to Dr O'Gooley for an appliance. I think I may have strapped it on the wrong way round as it is extremely painful.

Did you see M. giving her Mad Monk Memorial Lecture on the TV? Maurice rang me from the home to ask whether I'd like to book her in as there was a vacancy.

It all started with Dr Mulvany, McWhinnie? anyway that ghastly Ulsterman at Central Office, ringing us at Chester Square in advance to ask if they could have a transcript for their files. He was sure the old girl would not say anything controversial with an election looming and the Party trailing slightly in the polls. I could see a mad excited gleam come into the Boss's eye as she took the call, and she immediately refilled her glass while reassuring him that she would give her full support to her successor and promising to fax off something immediately. "Poor man," she crowed, draining the amber snort and winding a page from the telephone directory West London Residential A–C through the fax machine, "If only he knew who I meant by 'my successor'." With this she gave another harsh cackle and swayed from the room. It was some minutes before I twigged that she was referring to the unhinged robot from outer space with the funny eyes, Brer Redwood.

Come the opening night, needless to say, the Chief Dalek was there in the front row, accompanied by his little chums,

Lilley and Portillo, as prize a pair of bumlickers as I have seen outside of the Royal Opera House (as seen on TV), all clapping like mad. Margaret, fortified by a colossal overdose of the electric soup, raved on about the betrayal of the middle classes, all based I may say on a note from the Major about parking places in Tunbridge Wells and how he was going to vote for Blair.

Combined with her recent VG (Victory in the Gulf) Day Vera Lynn style comeback about why the hell they hadn't zapped Saddam while he was groggy and how Major had chickened out when it came to administering the killer punch, it all had a pretty destabilising effect at a time when O'Gooley has told her she ought to get as much rest as she can.

M. on such a high has always been a bit wearing, and things have not been made easier by the Boy Mark cropping up again in the blatts, his name linked this time to some buxom friend of Mrs Van der Kaffirbesher. I rang Mrs Van der K. to find out what the little sod was up to, but she was too upset about her better half having been sexually interfered with by one of the Rottweilers.

See you at Simpsons for the Saga Promotion. Bring a big bag and you can stock up on all the freebee miniatures the whisky fellows give away.

Yours, still clinging to the Zimmer,

DENIS

MARCH 1996

Dear Bill,

I must warn you that you will shortly be appearing in a work of fiction entitled "Denis Thatcher, The Missing Link, by His Daughter Carol". As you know, I've always had a soft spot for the girl ever since she pushed Mark off the top board at Broadstairs, and unlike the ghastly S and H she's never really had the hang of reeling in the spondulicks. Even when she got a job on the *Telegraph* that tall oaf Hastings gave her the bum's rush during a bout of downsizing. As the Canadian hoodlum with the leggy wife who owns the paper put it, "Hastings certainly knows how to drown the kittens." No great consolation for the girl Carol, you may say, who happened to be in the sack when he strode down at midnight to dump it from the Wharfside.

With Carol reduced to working for that shirt-lifter chappie who's on the wireless on Saturday mornings, I searched about a bit and came up with what I thought was a brilliant scheme. Having been dragged along on the Boss's coat-tails to some signing session in Peebles I had found myself in conversation with the fellow from HarperCollins, one Fishwick, who explained that all Carol really needed to do to make her fortune was to sign her name on the dotted, and a team of little monkeys would be set to work at the VDUs to produce a Book of the Month masterpiece the world had been waiting for.

All would have been well, but Carol, who likes the idea of herself as a bit of a journalist, insisted on interfering. The monkeys produced a perfectly good first draft, based on some tapes made late at night at the RAC, in which I reminisced about my wartime years, including the anecdote about Prosser-Cluff burning down the Mess in K.L. to show the natives who was boss, and a few thoughts about Brother Mandela letting the side down. I also dwelt at some length on the years at Burmah, enriching the tale with many amusing stories about Maurice and his gorilla suit.

Friend Fishwick perused all this, and said he liked it very much indeed, in fact he'd never enjoyed a first draft more in his whole experience of publishing. However, he wondered whether it wouldn't benefit from being a touch shorter and having "a bit of spin put on it", whatever that meant. He was afraid hostile pinko critics might run away with the idea that I was a sozzled half-wit of unacceptably right wing views.

This seemed fair enough, and Carol, who had always rather hankered to have a hand in it as she was named as the author, came up with the following wheeze. I don't know whether you've ever seen that show on the TV about the little man with glasses who goes into a telephone box and turns into Superman. Carol's idea was that I was such a man, only the other way round. In truth, a superhuman intellect, master of a hundred boardroom coups, capable of flying through the economic stratosphere and more than a match for Professor Walters and his tartan suitcases. Then, Shazam, I melt into the nearest telephone box and reappear as a shambling wino with a bag of golfclubs, the world no wiser as to my responsibility for shaping world events.

Carol has only quoted you very marginally on how you were convinced for many years by the success of my disguise.

Any chance of your coming to Fishwick's beano for the launch at the East India and Sports? Maurice is being let out with a minder, but unfortunately the major's extra testicle implant requested by the widow F. has gone seriously wrong and he may have to have a leg off.

Meanwhile I'm due to try out the new electric wheelchair at Huntercombe on Saturday — you may remember Maurice wrote off the last one going through the French windows of the clubhouse bar while escaping from his Air Malta Lady — and we could plan a jape or two to alarm the suits from HarperCollins.

Yours in print for £39.99,

DENIS

ALSO AVAILABLE FROM
PRIVATE EYE • CORGI

THE
PRIVATE EYE
ANNUAL
1996

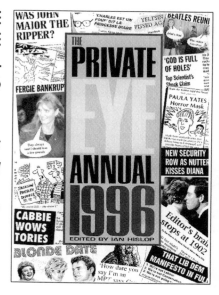

ALL THE
BEST FROM
PRIVATE EYE.
£6.99

COLEMANBALLS 8
Yet more unbelievable babble from Privaye Eye's long running column of cobblers.
£3.99

FUNNY OLD WORLD
Tales of the bizarre from the world's press.
£4.99